P9-AOT-867

The Gardens of SPAIN

The Gardens of

SPAIN

Photographs by Michael George
Text by Consuelo M. Correcher
Harry N. Abrams, Inc., Publishers

NOTE TO THE READER:

The botanical names of the following species are given here rather than in the text because they occur frequently: almond *(Prunus dulcis* var. *dulcis);* ash *(Fraxinus excelsior);* Atlas cedar *(Cedrus atlantica)*; belladonna lily *(Amaryllis Belladonna);* blue gum *(Eucalyptus Globulus);* bougainvillea *(Bougainvillea spectabilis);* boxwood *(Buxus sempervirens);* bridal wreath *(Spiraea* x *Vanhouttei)*; broom *(Cytisus strictus);* Canary Island date palm *(Phoenix canariensis);* cluster pine *(Pinus Pinaster);* cork oak *(Quercus Suber);* crape myrtle *(Lagestroemia indica);* date palm *(Phoenix dactylifera);* desert fan palm *(Washingtonia filifera);* European fan palm *(Chamaerops humilis);* European hazelnut *(Corylus Avellana);* heath *(Erica australis);* heather *(Calluna vulgaris);* hedge maple *(Acer campestre);* holly oak *(Quercus Ilex);* Italian cypress *(Cupressus sempervirens);* Italian stone pine *(Pinus pinea);* juniper *(Juniperus communis);* Kaffir lily *(Clivia miniata)*; laurel *(Laurus nobilis);* Monterey cypress *(Cupressus macrocarpa);* mountain ash *(Sorbus torminalis);* myrtle *(Myrtus communis);* oleander *(Nerium Oleander)*; olive *(Olea europaea);* rosemary *(Rosmarinus officinalis);* Seville orange tree *(Citrus Aurantium);* southern magnolia *(Magnolia grandiflora);* Spanish fir *(Abies Pinsapo)*; strawberry tree *(Arbutus Unedo);* sweet cherry *(Prunus avium);* thread palm *(Washingtonia robusta);* tulip tree *(Liriodendron Tulipifera)*; weeping willow *(Salix babylonica)*; white poplar *(Populus alba);* wild olive *(Olea europa* var. *Sylvestris);* and windmill palm *(Trachycarpus Fortunei).*

PAGE 1
Hortus Botanicus Marimurtra: The principal staircase, dedicated to Dr. P. Font y Quer

PAGE 2
Santa María de las Nieves: Rambling roses in the cloister garden

PAGE 3
La Majada del Lentisco: *Rosa Banksiae "Lutea"* in the principal patio

PAGES 4–5
Jardín de El Príncipe, Aranjuez: Salvia bed

PAGE 7
Torrebeleña: Roses climb a tree in a private garden in Madrid, belonging to Lino Llamas Madurga and Clara María González de Amezúa.

PAGE 8
Cloister Garden, Monasterio de San Lorenzo de Trasouto: A gardener pruning boxwood hedges

PAGE 9
Casa de Pilatos: Bougainvillea in the Jardín Grande

PAGES 20–21
Los Molinillos: The *patio de honor* and the house

PAGES 38–39
Los Palacios de Galiana: The *alberca*

PAGES 78–79
Palacio de Oca: The lower pond with its stone boat

PAGES 96–97
Santa Clotilde: View of the garden and the Mediterranean Sea

PAGES 114–115
S'Avall: The cactus garden

PAGES 124–125
Monforte: View toward the Romantic garden, with the Neoclassical garden in the foreground

PAGES 132–133
El Generalife: Twentieth-century gardens

All the photographs in this book were made with Olympus camera bodies and lenses. The photographer is indebted to Olympus America Inc for its generous assistance.

Translated by Wayne H. Finke

EDITOR: Eric Himmel
DESIGNER: Darilyn Lowe Carnes
Map by Christine Edwards

Library of Congress Cataloging-in-Publication Data
George, Michael, 1943–
The gardens of Spain/photographs by Michael George; text by Consuelo M. Correcher.
p. cm.
Includes index.
ISBN 0-8109-3370-5
1. Gardens—Spain. 2. Gardens—Spain—Pictorial works. I. Correcher, Consuelo M. II. Title
SB466.S7G46 1993
712'.0946—dc20 93-18305
CIP

Publisher in 1993 by Harry N. Abrams, Incorporated, New York
A Times Mirror Company

Printed and bound in Japan

Contents

Acknowledgments

THE PUBLICATION OF this book would not have been possible without the guidance and support of a number of individuals, chief among them my distinguished collaborator, Consuelo M. Correcher, whose valuable contribution of her unrivaled knowledge of Spanish horticulture is all the more generous, considering that the selection of gardens had already been made before she graciously undertook to write the accompanying text. Supportive from the outset were Lincoln Kirstein, who suggested to me at dinner in his house in Manhattan that I ought to consider a book on the gardens of Spain; Inmaculada de Habsburgo Lorena, then Director of the Spanish Institute, who first told me about the Palacio de Oca, where she had stayed as a guest of her cousin, Ignacio, Duke of Segorbe; and Francisco Giron, Director, and Pilar Vico, Public Relations Director, of the Tourist Office of Spain in New York, both of whom were extraordinarily kind and generous.

Subsequently, I received encouragement and assistance from so many people that I trust that those whose efforts on behalf of the book, among them the private owners of Spain's finest gardens, will accept in lieu of the paragraph or, in some cases, page, to which they may be entitled, the inadequate citation in the roll call of the acknowledgment that follows. At the same time, I hope that I may be forgiven by any person whose name I have inadvertently omitted. Finally, I should like to pay special tribute to my friends Elaine Markson and Geri Thoma of the Elaine Markson Literary Agency, Inc.

In Spain: José Juan Abrines, former Director, Patronato Provincial de Turismo de Costa del Sol; María Luisa Albacar, Director of Public Relations, Patronato Municipal de Turisme de Barcelona; Christopher González-Aller; Peggy González-Aller; Juan Antonio Bertran; José Elías Bonells, Director, Parques y Jardines, Ayuntamiento de Sevilla; Count and Countess of Bornos; Helena Cambó and Ramón Guardans; José Antonio del Canizo Perate, Director, Parques y Jardines Ayuntamiento de Málaga; Santiago Castroviejo, Director, Real Jardín Botánico de Madrid; Marchioness of Corvera; Sofía Domecq; Manuel Domecq-Zurita; Marquis and Marchioness of la Esperanza; Trinidad Jiménez-Lopera de Fierro; Margaret Gimson; Fernando Gómez Alcaína, Director, Parques y Jardines de Granada; Tomás Gómez Quesada, former Director, Patronato Provincial de Turismo de Granada; Felisa Hernández, Director of Public Relations, Patronato Municipal de Turismo de Sevilla; Gerald S. Huggan; Juan Joyanes, Director, Patronato Provincial de Turismo de Córdoba; Clara Maria González de Amezúa de Llamas; Kirk Long; Duchess of Mandas; Carmen Marañón de Fernández-Araoz; Bartolomé March Severa; José Marti, Director, Fundación de Jardines Singulares de Valencia; Jordi de Mas, Director, Parques/Jardines, Ayuntamiento de Barcelona; Countess of la Maza; Duchess of Medina de las Torres and of Soma; Marta Moriarty; Miguel de Oriol e Ybarra and Inés de Sarriera de Oriol; Francisco Páez de la Cadena; Iñaki Pagola; Patrimonio Nacional: Daniel Camina Carrasco, Director, *Real Sitio* of Aranjuez; Angel Fernández Cocero, Delegate, *Real Sitio* of La Granja de San Ildefonso; Pedro Criado Juárez, Director, *Real Sitio* of Monasterio de San Lorenzo el Real de El Escorial; Juan Pedrola Monfort, Director, Jardín Botánico, Marimurtra; Gerardo Quintana, former Director of Public Relations, Patronato Municipal de Turismo de Sevilla; Dr. Mateo Revilla, Director, Patronato de la Alhambra y Generalife; the family of the late Marchioness of Roviralta de Santa Clotilde; María José Ruíz, Public Relations, Patronato Provincial de Turismo de Granada; María de Salamanca, Countess Larisch; Duke of Segorbe; Leandro Silva Delgado and Julia Casaravilla; Montserrat Tortras Balcells, President, Los Amigos de Jardines, Barcelona; William Tucker; Nadine Ulloa; Piru de Urquijo; Alfonso Zobel de Ayala; Mary Melian Zobel; and Sylvia Melian de Zobel.

In New York: Paul Gottlieb, Publisher, President, Editor-in-Chief; Eric Himmel, Senior Editor; and Darilyn Lowe Carnes, Senior Designer, all of Harry N. Abrams Inc.; Douglas Brenner; Dudley P. Frasier; Elena Garrigues; Donald L. Hillegas; Timothy S. Jensen; Anthony Korner, Publisher, *Artforum International;* Pamela Lord, Editorial Consultant, the Garden Book Club; Ada Marina Newman, Public Relations, Tourist Office of Spain; Denise Otis; David Parker, Esq., Kleinberg, Kaplan, Wolff & Cohen, P. C.; Catherine Powis, Librarian, the Horticultural Society of New York; Oscar de la Renta; William S. Rieder, Associate Curator, European Sculpture and Decorative Arts, the Metropolitan Museum of Art; Elizabeth Barlow Rogers, Central Park Administrator; Jill Rose, President of the Board of Trustees, the International Center of Photography; José Suárez, Manager, 380 Copy Services; and Marcia T. Thompson, Vice Chairman, National Arts Stabilization Fund.

Michael George

Castillo de Layos: Hydrangeas on the ledge of the well in the patio

Introduction

Occupying the greater part of the Iberian peninsula, Spain projects itself between two seas that have been of great importance to the history of humanity: the Atlantic Ocean and the Mediterranean Sea, in both of which its territory is complemented by islands—the Canaries in the former, the Balearics in the latter. To the ancient Greeks, who explored the Mediterranean and settled its shores, Spain, which they called Hesperia, was at the end of the world. There, they envisioned a wondrous garden, in which a tree bore the golden apples that Hera received as a gift from the Mother Goddess Gaia upon her marriage to Zeus. They called it the Garden of Hesperides, a word meaning "the nymphs of the evening," after the maidens who guarded this mythic place, which some scholars locate in Spain. Let us begin by invoking, as an emblem of Spain's intense allegiance to ancient tradition, the name of this legendary first garden.

Now let us cross the millennia to the sixteenth century, when Atlantic Spain was, in a sense, the beginning of the world; opening up the New World to Europe and colonizing large regions of the Americas. King Philip II (1556–98), the ruler of the largest empire the world had ever seen, who took a passionate interest in horticulture, created in Aranjuez a garden, today in a lamentable state of decay, that was to be "the model of world gardens."

Between the heritage of the Old World and the unexpected discoveries of the New, we will find the keys to unlock the gardens of Spain.

Like all high plateaus in temperate regions, the *meseta* endures severe winters and fiery summers. To delight the eyes and gladden the spirit, nature compensates with a veritable explosion of flowers in the springtime, which lasts at most a month. Along the embankments of roads and even highways wild charlock, poppies, and mallows struggle to grow and then proudly flourish. Who could better arrange a mixed border?

OPPOSITE

The Romans bequeathed to Spain the patio, an open space in the center of the house, often enclosed by galleries. The neat, sober marble patios of the old city of Seville make a strong contrast with the more open, cheerful patios of Córdoba: here, one is in the realm of aspidistras, chessboard patterns on the floor, and burnished copper pots, while life seems banished to the shadows.

An olive tree and a holly oak grow in the stony ground at Santa María de las Nieves, on the *meseta* not far from Toledo.

Continental Spain, approximately the size of California plus about one-third of Nevada, embraces extreme variations in climate, ranging from the eternal snows of the high *sierras*; to the humid, temperate northern provinces; to the arid *meseta*, the high central plateau that occupies almost three-quarters of the land-area of the country, with its freezing winters and broiling summers; to the subtropical Mediterranean coast. Against a great floral variety of more than eight thousand species must be weighed the relatively narrow range of indigenous trees and shrubs. The main species of the typical climax environment in Spain, that is, of the final stage of ecological succession, are the holly oak, called *encina* in Spanish, and its court (cork oak, English oak, and others), and the olive and wild olive, or *acebuche*. The evergreen holly oak rarely reaches great size but is virtually ageless: Pliny (A.D. 61–c. 113) believed that specimens growing in Rome predated the founding of the city. The olive, another small tree of legendary longevity, was possibly introduced to Spain by the Phoenicians at the end of the second millennium B.C. From our secure vantage point in the late twentieth century, it is all too easy to overlook the contribution made to human well-being over the course of thousands of years by these trees.

We find them throughout Spain. In the *sierras* surrounding El Castañar, they grow amid such familiar trees as juniper, pine, hedge maple, mountain ash, European ash, almond, sweet cherry, English walnut, strawberry tree, and European hazelnut. They are also the main species of the maquis, the low, scrubby environment typical of the Mediterranean basin, a characteristic example of which is preserved in the garden at Marimurtra. River valleys support gallery forests, with the characteristic presence of elm and poplar groves, as at Brihuega, where the Río Tajuña flows past the Real Fábrica de Paños.

We can understand the evolution of a Spanish garden tradition largely as the consequence of cultural—and, hence, political—events unfolding on this stage provided by nature. Modern Spain was created by the diverse peoples that traversed the Mediterranean, crossed the Strait of Gibraltar that links Europe and Africa, and—more rarely—scaled the towering Pyrenees. From the south and the east came Iberians, Phoenicians, Greeks, Carthaginians, Romans, Arabs, Berbers, and Jews; from the north Celts, Vandals, Suevi, Alani, and Visigoths.

Two civilizations in particular left their mark on the peninsula, transmitting to it the legacy of their gardens: seven centuries of Roman hegemony (205 B.C.–c. A.D. 500) was followed by eight centuries of Moorish occupation (711–1492), which only ended when Granada, the last Moorish stronghold on Iberian soil, fell to the Christian forces of the kingdoms of Castile and Aragón. Nor are the contri-

butions of the Jews to the land that they called Sefarad to be overlooked. Spain's greatest achievement before the Reconquest and the expulsions of its two most dynamic communities, the Moors and the Jews, was the creation of a pluralistic society, in which art, literature, and science flourished with the harmonious coexistence of the three peoples. And even today, Spain is a kaleidoscope, making beautiful images from a jumble of unmatched pieces.

We do not need to resort to archaeology, which no doubt will yield vestiges of splendid gardens in Mérida, Segóbriga, Italica, and so many other sites throughout the peninsula, to see the impact of the Roman presence on Spanish horticulture. Equally at home in country and city, the Romans established the prototypical Spanish garden space, the patio, adapting the peristyle that they had borrowed from the Greeks. Ornamental gardening flourished at the heart of the Roman villa, the *hortus*: these vast, self-sufficient estates, with their fruit and vegetable gardens, established land use patterns that in some cases, as at the Castillo de Layos, persist up to the present day.

Under the Moors, al-Andalus, as Islamic Spain was called, eclipsed the rest of Europe as *the* center of civilization. In the realms of agriculture, horticulture, and medicine, its scholars not only preserved the classics by translating Greek texts; they also advanced their knowledge through experimentation and fieldwork, which they then wrote up in treatises. Among those who considered the aesthetics of garden design was Ibn Layun, who described the ideal house with garden. The Moors absorbed the knowledge of other civilizations besides the Greek, and of inestimable value was Nabatean horticulture, acquired by the Arabs when they conquered Persia and applied by them in Spain to the cultivation and irrigation of fruit trees.

The impact of the Islamic achievement in agriculture and horticulture is visible throughout Spain today, in the form of terraced plots that are separated by walls of verdure and stucco, watered by canals and fountains, and planted with fruit and vegetable species mixed with ornamentals and the evergreen species that were so dear to the Moors. In addition, in the Alhambra and the Generalife in Granada, Spain still possesses the most beautiful Islamic palace gardens, which were designed to gratify the eternal need for transcendental experience. In Córdoba, the oldest enclosed garden in Europe, the ninth-century Patio de los Naranjos in the Great Mosque, continues to be a sacred place in which people of different faiths today seek spiritual renewal.

That the Great Mosque contains in its heart a cathedral is, of course, a consequence of the Reconquest, which was successfully completed in 1492 by the

Nowhere in Spain is its mixed cultural heritage more pronounced than at the Reales Alcazares in Seville, a Christian palace largely built by Islamic craftsmen under the direction of Hispanic architects. The tiled pavilion of Charles V was built in the gardens in 1543, almost certainly on the site of an earlier Arabic pavilion, or *qubba,* hence the name of this part of the garden: Alcoba. Groves of orange, lemon, and citron trees surround the pavilion, explaining the presence of the nearby *alberca,* or irrigation pool, of Arabic origin.

Catholic Monarchs, King Ferdinand II of Aragón (1452–1516) and Queen Isabella I of Castile (1451–1504). Of Christian gardens made before that date, there are not many left in Spain. The Gothic castle (c. 1400–19) of the kings of Navarre in Olite was reputed to have luxurious hanging gardens, of which nothing now remains. In medieval Christian Spain, monasteries, like the Monasterio de Poblet in Vimbodí, were the repositories of horticultural knowledge; its growth, however, was a consequence of the Renaissance itself, which stimulated interest both in classical and empirical science. In Spain, this meant in practice the Christian assimilation of Islamic scholarship: the epochal publication in 1513 of the *Libro de agricultura general* by Gabriel Alonso de Herrera would not have been possible without the tenth-century medical encyclopedia of Abu'l-Qasim al-Zahrawi.

It is to this multicultural synthesis in the sixteenth century that the most powerful nation in the world owed such great gardens as the Patio de los Evangelistas in the Escorial, which, some people may be surprised to learn, originally had a marvelous floral variety—some sixty-eight species were counted in 1592—of Hispano-Islamic tradition. The more human side of its complex creator, Philip II, who bore the full weight of Spain's global empire on his shoulders, was reflected in his passionate interests in the study of botany, the creation of gardens, and, above all, in the cultivation of flowers, which delighted him (his favorite was the musk rose). The botanist Francisco Hernández sent Philip plants gathered in the Americas, while Jerónimo de Algora was dispatched to study gardens in other European countries; under Philip's patronage the royal physician Andrés Laguna (c. 1499–1560) published his translation of Dioscorides's *De materia medica* (c. A.D. 77), essentially the first practical herbal in the Spanish vernacular; and the king encouraged Gregorio de los Ríos to write a treatise of aesthetics and garden design, *Agricultura de jardines,* in 1592.

The influence of the Renaissance on the Spanish garden was reinforced by the Habsburg monarchs' possessions in Italy (Milan, Naples, and Sicily): newly fashionable classical statuary ornamented its paths, complementing the topiary hedges first introduced by the Romans, the displays of water, and the colorful, aromatic floral plantings of Islamic tradition. To these various elements, of course, we must add the botanical contributions of the New World, for Spain was the first country to welcome numerous species to Europe, among them potatoes, corn, quinine, magnolia, and dahlia, as it had Asian species in the preceding centuries.

The eighteenth century was a happy one for Spanish gardens. The complete works of the great Swedish father of botany Carolus Linnaeus (1707–1778) were first translated into Spanish in 1784 by the Catalan botanist and plantsman Antonio Palau y Verdera. Linnaeus called Spain the "garden of the orb" and sent his favorite pupil Petrus Löfling to Spain to make an inventory of its species, while Spanish botanists like José Celestino Mutis (1732–1808) and Antonio José Cavanilles (1745–1804) gained world renown. Spain's Bourbon kings gave a fresh impetus to horticulture, encouraging botanical expeditions to their colonies in America and Asia and establishing botanical gardens for the acclimation and propagation of new species. In Madrid, the Real Jardín Botánico was founded by King Charles III (1759–88) in his unceasing attempt to civilize and improve his capital. Also dating from this period is the Jardín de Aclimatación de La Orotava on the island of Tenerife in the Canaries, the Jardín Botánico of Valencia, and the Jardín de El Príncipe in Aranjuez. Following the example of royalty, the aristocracy commissioned gardens throughout Spain, among them El Capricho , La Moncloa, El Laberinto de Horta, El Retiro de Churriana, Raixa, Liria, El Jardín de Gourié, Bertiz: some have survived the vicissitudes of time, some have not.

In the courtly, scientific, and private gardens of the late eighteenth century, a balance seems to have been achieved between the two dominant tendencies of European art, Neoclassicism and Romanticism. Throughout Europe in the nineteenth century Romanticism finally triumphed, and it is interesting to see in such gardens as the Real Fábrica de Paños and the Jardines de Narváez how the Isabeline

Less than six miles northeast of Madrid is the three-hundred-and-seventy-acre country estate of El Capricho, which once belonged to the Dukes of Osuna. The extraordinary María Josefa Alonso–Pimentel y Téllez–Girón, Countess-Duchess of Benavente by birth and Duchess of Osuna by marriage, desired to possess a garden corresponding to her philosophical, artistic, and botanical ideas, and to that end, she reserved thirty-seven acres that were walled and separated from the rest of the estate; employed a series of Spanish and French gardeners between 1784 and 1795; and obtained exotic plants from Paris, London, and the king's own gardens in Madrid and Aranjuez. The garden was ornamented with elaborate follies in a classicizing or rustic vein, to which the Duchess's son later added a miniature fortress, with moat, drawbridge, cannon, and soldiers that were activated mechanically. El Capricho was acquired by the Ayuntamiento Municipal de Madrid in 1977 and is slowly being restored.

The nineteenth-century *ensanche,* or enlargement, of Barcelona changed the face of the old city. The Cerdà Plan of 1859 called for a network of streets that soon became entire neighborhoods of apartment houses for the rising middle classes of Catalonia. These dignified buildings are early examples of modern architecture, devoting an ever-increasing surface area of the main façade to windows. Many apartments had wrought-iron balconies that have given rise, even where tenants have occupied them for generations, to nostalgic recreations of the patios and gardens of an ever-receding rural past.

style in furnishings and fashion, named for Queen Isabella II (1830–1904), found expression.

By the end of the nineteenth century, the introduction of plants from abroad had permanently modified the plantings of the Spanish garden. The cypress, oak, and olive that are so typical of the Mediterranean region have had to yield to species from afar. Galicia, where the first camellia arrived only in the late eighteenth century, is now firmly identified with that Asian tree, which grows there along with magnolias from North America and pines from Australia. The geranium that originally came from South Africa is now virtually the principal flower of southern Spain.

The twentieth century began with the creation of a unique garden that deserves to be better known: Barcelona's Parque Güell (1900–14), a monument to the imagination and passion of its creator, Antonio Gaudí (1852–1926), the genius of Modernism. Unfortunately, the century, now nearly at an end, has not been kind to Spanish gardens. The 1920s and 1930s saw the creation of many gardens that mistook a superficial historicism for the true Spanish spirit. There were voices in the desert: Rubió y Tudurí, the landscape architect; Winthuysen, the theoretician; Durán-Loriga, the architect; and later the Marchioness of Casa Valdés, the great chronicler of gardens, whose own garden at Piedras Menaras is included here. However, from the 1940s to the 1960s the Spanish garden, with its complex heritage blending ancient Roman, Islamic, and medieval Christian traditions, was overwhelmed by the indiscriminate planting of lawns. Authentic Spanish gardens lost their bowers of shade; their delicate and fragrant borders of violets, roses, and lilies; their pear, apple, pomegranate, almond, and orange trees; their seemingly sempiternal walnuts, chestnuts, oaks, pines, and elms; their towering cypresses and palms. The courtly Renaissance and Baroque gardens of the sixteenth and seventeenth centuries befit a golden age, the sophisticated gardens of the Age of Enlightenment expressed the reigning values of their time, and the poetic nineteenth-century Romantic garden concentrated the despair of a hundred years of invasions, wars, and disasters. The gardens of the twentieth century have been, for the most part, silent.

Happily, in the last twenty-five years there has been a stirring in Spain, a revival of interest in the concept of the garden as the work, not of nature, but of men and women, and a new comprehension of its essence. The true Spanish gardener, involved in a spiritual quest, does not strive for material wealth but, through a grounding in Spain's two-thousand-year-old gardening tradition, seeks unity in infinite variety. This aesthetic is based on a multiplicity of ideas and materials, among which the most important may be defined as: a pronounced horizontality in composition; a rhythmical planting of trees in rows; a corpus of trimmed hedges; a faint sound of water; a reflection of light off water; a pervading fragrance; a seasonal presence of color; and an ultimate sense of enclosure.

A roadside garden near Fornalutx on Majorca: the typical Majorcan mortarless stone wall, in which the larger stones are at the bottom to make the structure more stable, seems to be holding back, with little apparent success, an overflowing of perpetual flowering climbing cranesbill. Behind the wall, a humble orchard of orange trees separates the house from the highway, while a cypress tree on the edge of the property serves, as it has since Roman times, as a sign of hospitality. Century plants casually guard the wall. This can be classed as a Mediterranean garden in which plants from China, Persia, Mexico, and South Africa are quite at home. All ships dock at an island, and itinerant plants take root in a garden.

Madrid

Patio de los Evangelistas, Monasterio de San Lorenzo el Real de El Escorial

Patrimonio Nacional–Real Casa

PHILIP II ORDERED the construction of the monastery-residence of San Lorenzo el Real de El Escorial, which would also serve as the last resting place for his parents, the Holy Roman Emperor Charles V (Charles I of Spain, 1517–56) and Doña Isabel of Portugal. He named it in fulfillment of a vow that he made on the battlefield of Saint Quentin in 1557, and he commissioned as architects, first, Juan Bautista de Toledo, then Juan de Herrera, frequently looking over the plan, which may have been designed to represent the gridiron always associated with the martyrdom of the saint to whom the greatest building enterprise of his reign was dedicated. The Escorial was built about thirty miles northwest of Madrid, at the foot of the Sierra de Guadarrama, on a solid granite base, where there was good air and plentiful water.

Great care was taken in siting the building so that it would receive maximum exposure to the sun as well as protection from the cold mountain winds. This ensured the good health of both the Hieronymite monks and the plants in the gardens on the south and east terraces and within the private precincts of the patio created for the exclusive use of the religious community. The largest of fourteen courtyards contained within the Escorial, the Patio de los Evangelistas, on the south side of the chapel, was provided with a garden for the monks' contemplation and recreation. Catholic symbolism predominates in this patio, which expresses the religiosity of the king, who was defender of the faith during the Counter-Reformation.

The patio was designed in the Renaissance style as a perfect square, with the galleries on each side carried by twelve Doric pilasters, an allusion to Christ's apostles. Numerology is certainly appropriate to this space, divided as it is by two paths crossing at the center and then further subdivided by four paths that create a grid of sixteen squares and many crosses. The four squares in the middle contain pools, forming a parterre of water; the twelve surrounding squares are parterres with clipped hedges.

In the center, an octagonal domed pavilion was built over the crossing of the paths, with sculptures of the four evangelists in niches in the blind sides, from which water flows into the pools below. With the Patio de los Evangelistas, the architects succeeded in transforming the Renaissance garden with its pagan and mythological symbols into a Christian *Hortus Conclusus,* in which, in accordance with the Counter-Reformation principles of the Council of Trent, primacy was given to the word of Christ as transmitted by the Gospels.

Among Philip II's gardeners were Friar Marcos de Cardona, Juan Anglés, Jerónimo de Algora, and the Holveque brothers, who worked in the different gardens of the monastery. It is a little-known fact that the beds in the Patio de los Evangelistas, which were surrounded by hedges of lavender *(Santolina Chamaecyparissus)* and myrtle brought specially from Talavera de la Reina, were once planted with a variety of flowering plants. The flowers listed by Juan Alonso de Almela in 1592 comprise some sixty-eight species, which may be grouped in three categories: medicinal plants, plants used for decoration and perfumes, and the recently introduced plants sent from the Americas by the botanist Francisco Hernández.

Over time, the Hispano-Arabic legacy of the garden, with its many fragrant and colorful flowers, was erased. The great fire of 1671 badly damaged the garden. Little by little the plantings were replaced with boxwood, an indigenous plant from the Serrania de Cuenca, which now occupies all the parterres around the pools and is accepted as being in harmony with the monument's austere elevations. If time, the transformer of all things, has altered the original garden, this possible loss of authenticity has its compensations, and when the sun causes the boxwood to release its penetrating fragrance, the Patio de los Evangelistas is transmuted into an immense incensory.

Los Molinillos: The pansy bed adjoining the terrace

Los Molinillos: The *patio de honor* from the house

THE 1,200 ACRE estate of Los Molinillos is located some twenty miles northwest of Madrid on the Castilian *meseta*, the high central plateau that occupies almost three-quarters of the land area of Spain. Los Molinillos was originally a dependency of the nearby Monasterio de San Lorenzo de El Escorial and its rents supported the Hieronymite community there. On the stream crossing the property, a tributary of the Río Perales where today ash trees can be seen along its banks, water-driven fulling mills that gave the estate its name ("The Little Mills") were installed in the second half of the sixteenth century to beat the wool that was its main product.

The property was purchased in 1939 as a hunting lodge by Jaime de Urquíjo's father, the Marquess of Amurrio. Some of the heaviest fighting in the Civil War took place here, completely destroying the nearby town of Brunete. The main house at Los Molinillos, which served as a headquarters for both armies, suffered terrible damage and was rebuilt in the early 1940s by a California architect named Arthur E. Mid-

LOS MOLINILLOS

Brunete
Jaime de Urquíjo and Carmen
Fernández de Araoz

Los Molinillos: Entrance to the enclosed patio from the garden

dlehurst, who specialized in the restoration of old Spanish missions. It is a traditional dwelling, with shuttered windows and wrought-iron balustrades, constructed around a patio with a central fountain that is screened from the property by an arcade. The front porch is where the family can relax and entertain friends who come to hunt.

The low ridge on which the Urquíjos built affords sweeping views of the surrounding Castilian landscape of rolling hills dotted with holly oaks. The laying out of the garden, which covers almost five acres on two sides of the house, was entrusted to Cecilio Rodríguez, at that time the head gardener of Madrid. It is considered one of his most successful creations.

Entering the *patio de honor*, the garden in front of the house, the visitor is impressed by the main compositional element, the hedging of Monterey cypress, trimmed with geometric precision, that lines the circular drive and the secondary paths, and by the handsome specimens of smooth cypress *(Cupressus glabra)*, Italian cypress, Atlas cedar, and southern magnolia. The species that lends character to the garden is the lilac, popular around the turn of the century in the flower gardens of the Madrid aristocracy.

Running the full length of the front of the house is a pebble-and-brick-paved terrace enclosed by a broad bed densely planted with European wild pansies *(Viola tricolor)*, a Spanish gardening tradition of ten centuries or more, interplanted with towering Italian cypresses. This part of the garden framing the principal entrance receives the particular attention of the American horticulturist Bill Tucker, working in close consultation with Carmen Fernández de Araoz, who is known to her friends

as Piru. The front porch, a groin-vaulted loggia, has dark green furniture and is decorated with spruces in saucer-shaped pots. There is a reminiscence of the Andalusian *cortijo* in the enclosed courtyard with its central fountain and view of a high Castilian hill at the rear of the house. At its four corners Piru Urquíjo has planted bright red azaleas *(Rhododendron indicum)* in pots.

To the east, a large garden opens out. The terraced ground descends gently to a path edged with powerful hedging of Monterey cypress, punctuated by taller crape myrtles *(Lagestroemia indica)* planted at regular intervals, that overlooks what was once a large *rosaleda,* a specialty of Cecilio Rodríguez, who was inspired by Forestier's rose garden at Bagatelle in Paris to create a similar one for the Retiro in Madrid. Years ago, the present owners transformed this rose garden into a large lawn that leads, on a lower level, to an area occupied by a central pool and that is surrounded by well-maintained sandy paths bordered by hedges that rise and link in beautiful arches. Elsewhere, there are a greenhouse for raising indoor plants for the house; a cutting garden for Piru Urquíjo's floral arrangements; and an area for seedlings, from which are "pricked out" the hundreds of pansies in the big border in front of the house.

The countryside surrounding Los Molinillos teems with game, and the visitor who strolls along its garden paths may encounter a hare or a partridge. A half-hour walk from the house takes one to the stream, where an enormous ash shades a granite, oval-shaped table and four benches, of unknown date, called the Mesa del Chocolate. Would the monks' emissaries have been entertained there with small cups of chocolate when they came to collect the rent?

Los Molinillos: The enclosed patio from the house

Los Molinillos: View to the east; looking from the terrace toward the pool

Los Molinillos: The garden with pool

SOME THIRTY YEARS ago, the first private house was built on land bordering the Monte de El Pardo, the former *cazadero,* or hunting ground, of the kings of Spain some eight miles northwest of Madrid, above the Río Manzanares, which timidly winds its way toward the capital. Appropriately, the house was named La Mirada, meaning "the view," because of its favored situation. Today, the large, leafy suburb of Puerta de Hierro overlooks the vast panorama that so moved Velázquez, a wide landscape crowned by the bluish barrier of the Sierra de Guadarrama range, whose highest snowcapped peaks glitter in the sunlight.

The house at La Mirada (designed by Madrid architect Luis Gutiérrez Soto) accommodates itself to the slope, with one story at the front and two at the rear, overlooking a large lawn sheltered by tall trees. Trini Fierro's exquisite taste is clearly manifest in her preference for white flowers, among them April-flowering bridal wreath and the May-flowering cranberry bush *(Viburnum Opulus).* The terrace, protected from the afternoon sun by an awning, is an open-air salon, elegantly decorated with blue and white cast-iron flowerpots brought from France, from which emerge conical shapes of ivy and laurel.

The design of the garden was entrusted to Mirambel, an eminent gardener from Catalonia, when there were few professional landscape architects in Spain. Today, the garden receives the constant attention of the lady of the house who, with the assistance of landscape gardener Gerald Huggan, has recently made several modifications to Mirambel's design. It should be noted that a single gardener cares for the entire five acres. The uneven terrain has been utilized with excellent results: its hills and hollows provide for the volumetric play necessary to the aesthetic of the post-Romantic garden. The sandy paths invite strolling and hint—with a certain mystery—at what is not visible, creating zones of intimacy. The eclectic planting, most notably the tall conifers, is now, after thirty years, reaching maturity: like the magnolias, the great pines and cedars were brought from Catalonia as part of the original project. Most of the cedars are Atlas cedars; one of these splendid specimens, forty-five feet tall, is the rarer blue variety, *Cedrus atlantica "Glauca."*

Set in a lawn to the north of the house is a swimming pool in the classical style, shaded by a large weeping willow. At the far end four stone columns create an exedra that harmonizes perfectly with the Roman ambience. From here, a grand flight of steps descends between hedges of cherry laurel *(Prunus Laurocerasus),* magnificent specimens from a palace on the Paseo de la Castellana, until recently Madrid's most aristocratic avenue, which also provided the two antique wrought-iron lamps that mark the entrance to the property. Set into the rear wall of an open

La Mirada

Madrid
Alfonso Fierro Viña and
Trinidad Jiménez–Lopera de
Fierro

La Yedra

Madrid
Juan Carlos Fierro and Sofía
Domecq

La Mirada: Irises

La Mirada: The garden façade and terrace

OPPOSITE ABOVE
La Mirada: The exedra

OPPOSITE BELOW
La Yedra: The main lawn

pavilion by the pool is a Roman mosaic, discovered in Córdoba, whose ocher and sienna tesserae form a geometric backdrop for late-twentieth-century socializing.

It is with some surprise that one discovers, at the foot of the stairs, another garden, surrounding the house of Juan Carlos Fierro and his family. La Yedra (the Spanish word for "ivy," from the Latin *hedera)* possesses an exquisite *rosaleda.* Sofía Domecq de Urquíjo, whose husband's parents own La Mirada, belongs on her maternal side to a family for generations linked with roses. Her grandmother, the Marchioness of Urquíjo, gave her name to a large yellow rose tinged with ochre and orange hues hybridized by Cipriano Camprubí Nadal of Hospitalet, near Barcelona, in 1938. A cutting rose, it was awarded prizes in London and Paris, and for twenty years was one of the queens of roses. (In the United States this rose is also known by the name Pilar Landecho.) Sofía's aunt Blanca de Urquijo y Landecho is one of Spain's greatest connoisseurs of roses; she donated one of her collections of antique roses to the Real Jardín Botánico in Madrid. In Sofía Domecq's rose garden at La Yedra there are many famous antique roses, which were once difficult to obtain but have come back into fashion.

CALLE TURÉGANO, 1

Madrid
Jesús Huarte and Marta
Moriarty

THE PRIVATE RESIDENCE of Jesús Huarte, a well-known developer, was built some thirty years ago by the prominent modern architects José Antonio Corrales and Ramón Vázquez Molezún. To guide them they had Marian Jiménez Altolaguirre, the then wife of Huarte and the mother of their four children. Her impeccable taste provided the inspiration for the remarkably free treatment of space that characterizes both the house and the garden that were built in 1965.

Seen from afar, the house, whose principal construction materials are brick and ceramic tiles of a warm, dark hue, rises like a living being, so completely does it break away from the conventions of residential architecture otherwise observed in affluent Puerta de Hierro's leafy community of traditional dwellings. The architects were no doubt influenced in the final balance of exterior and interior space—here handled as a seamless whole—by the lady of the house's southern instinct for living out of doors. They took full advantage of the corner site, and the discreet street entrance to the house gives no clue to the way in which its interiors flow inevitably, through large floor-to-ceiling sliding glass doors, into a complementary suite of self-contained but interconnected outdoor garden rooms, curtained and carpeted with green foliage and grass, and wrapped around its two sheltered sides.

In the principal garden carefully terraced landings rise in grassy planes, and the adjoining brick wall of the house is cloaked with a thick vine. Steep embankments on its two outer edges converge beneath the rustling leaves of poplar trees that enclose a garden of pansies, narcissus, hyacinths, magnolias, photinias, strawberry trees, hollies, plum trees, hydrangeas, camellias, azaleas, bergenias, strawberries, and roses. It was in this corner that Marta Moriarty, who runs one of the leading

art galleries in Madrid and who married Jesús Huarte after the death of his first wife, recently decided to launch contemporary sculpture in this garden by giving pride of place to a monumental work in bronze by Jorge Oteiza, the celebrated Basque sculptor. On the raised lawn, subtly nuanced shafts of gleaming white marble, sculpted by Carlos Ferreira, add their vertical, abstract presence to the horizontally tiered green space and, in a fashion that is reminiscent of Moorish gardens, three incised roundels of white marble set flush with the manicured surface of the central lawn raise faint jets of water.

At the high corner of this garden area, a terrace planted with honeysuckle serves as a footbridge over the kitchen roof connecting the formal "reception area," as it were, with the more intimate garden room, also accessible through one of the bedrooms, that is a personal favorite of Marta Moriarty. Here, a pocket-handkerchief terrace of brick next to the house offers a relaxing vantage point to enjoy a small garden where a great weeping willow and a catalpa *(C. bignonioides)* shade a spiky metal abstraction by Ferreira and there are fountains in the form of roundels of Porriño granite set in the lawn. Boxwood, peonies, laurel, clematis, and a mimosa in one corner complete the ensemble.

Enclosed by these two garden "wings," and entered via the sliding glass doors of the house, is the solarium, a paved patio, partly shaded by a wisteria-clad pergola and bordered on one side by a raised pool, whose lining of cobalt blue tiles is brilliantly accented by a bank of honeysuckle planted atop its rear wall. The generous low shelf that separates the patio from the pool is used for an informal exhibition of several small contemporary bronze sculptures.

Calle Turégano, 1: The pergola in the solarium

OPPOSITE
Calle Turégano, 1: The pool in the solarium

Calle Turégano, 1: The garden adjoining the principal bedroom

ARANJUEZ, TWENTY-NINE miles south of Madrid, has been favored by royalty since the reign of the Catholic Monarchs. It combines the natural beauty of its situation in the valley of the Río Tajo with the beauty created by man: splendid avenues of trees and remarkable gardens. Among its many wonders we find the Jardín de El Príncipe, which owes its name to the Prince of Asturias, later King Charles IV (1788–1808).

Its history can be traced to medieval times, when there were *huertas* here irrigated by waterwheels and gristmills on the riverbank. Until the end of the Middle Ages, the Castilian language had only one word for garden: *huerto,* and its alternative form, *huerta,* indicating a larger estate, from the Latin *hortus.* Since virtually all gardens in both Christian and Moorish Spain had a productive function, it was only during the Renaissance that the term *huerto de placer,* or pleasure garden, was introduced, and even later that the word *jardín,* borrowed from the French, became interchangeable with *huerto* and *huerta.* Often rendered in English as "orchard," these terms actually embrace a particularly Spanish form of garden, in which fruit, vegetables, and ornamentals were grown.

The oldest recorded tract was situated between the *Sotillo,* a small grove along the river, and the old road from Colmenar de Oreja in the east. It had become known as the Huerta, or Jardín, de la Primavera by the time Ferdinand VI used it as a departure point for afternoon hunts and as the setting for evening concerts beside the river for Queen Bárbara de Braganza, and when Charles III subsequently gave the land to his son and heir, it became the nucleus for the garden the prince created with his favorite architect, Juan de Villanueva, a genius of the Neoclassical school, and his gardener, Pablo Boutelou, born in Aranjuez of French ancestry.

Without disturbing the basic layout of the Jardín de la Primavera, they planned a garden presided over by Minerva and Pomona. It is here that we find in perfect balance enlightened despotism's maxim "utility is beauty" and the quest for human liberty in all its physical and spiritual dimensions. The example of the English landscape garden was influential, as were the traditions of the Chinese garden, insofar as they were then known. Spanish and other botanists, who were protected by the Spanish crown on their scientific expeditions, gathered and sent back to the Iberian peninsula exotic species to form an extraordinary collection, of which still exist such trees as bald cypress *(Taxodium distichum* var. *distichum),* tulip tree, Norway maple *(Acer platanoides),* sugar maple *(A. saccharum),* old man's beard *(Chionanthus virginicus),* persimmon *(Diospyros virginiana),* and many others.

A world of fantasy was created, a paradise fit for habitation by Apollo and Narcissus, Ceres and Hercules. As if by magic, pagodas, pavilions, and obelisks sprouted among the rare trees, fields of carnations, and dahlia forests, where the flowers grew to seven feet. To the wonderment of the courtiers, there grew in this garden both bignonias and passionflowers, to say nothing of the renowned asparagus and the succulent strawberries for which this region is so famous. The fruit of sixty species of pears, thirty different apples, fifty varieties of peaches, and innumerable types of grape fell upon the paths of this garden. All this served for the delectation of kings and princes, who also ordered the construction of two follies, the Casa del Ermitaño and the Casa del Labrador: the former was a replica of a humble hermitage with a servant playacting the role of a hermit, the latter, hardly a laborer's cottage, was actually a sumptuous little palace.

The Jardín de El Príncipe, more than two hundred years old, could be considered as a prime example of a Spanish garden. Yet it would appear that the poet who wrote about "fields of solitude, languid hills" was referring to the dismal scene that greets the visitor to Aranjuez today. That these once spectacular royal gardens have been permitted to deteriorate is indicative of the place that monumental gardens hold in the consideration of our artistic and historic heritage.

JARDÍN DE EL PRÍNCIPE

Aranjuez
Patrimonio Nacional–Real Casa

Jardín de El Príncipe: Apollo

OPPOSITE
Jardín de El Príncipe: The allée leading to the Fuente de Apollo

Castile

Piedras Menaras

Guadalajara
Count and Countess of Bornos

Piedras Menaras: A stone lion guards a
mixed border

OPPOSITE
Piedras Menaras: The *rosaleda*

Tʜᴇ ʜɪɢʜ ᴄᴀsᴛɪʟɪᴀɴ plateau is characterized by extreme temperatures in winter
and summer: winds sweep the *meseta,* rainfall is sparse, and even the casual
observer notes that plants flower a month later than in Madrid. In the area
known as the Alcarria, east of Madrid, almost three thousand feet above sea level,
the Río Tajo flows through limestone clefts and melliferous plants grow on the
mountain slopes. Here is the estate of Monte Alcarria, which, when it passed by
inheritance to the Marquess of Casa Valdés at the beginning of this century, consisted of some 14,800 acres of uninhabited land: every fourteen years one of its fourteen sections was virtually leveled; the indigenous oak trees were felled for the
firewood and charcoal so necessary in such a harsh climate.

After the Civil War, Don Juan Valdés decided to use part of the estate for cereal production and sheep farming. Where the soil favored agriculture, the fields were
plowed, though without cutting down the largest holly oaks. This no doubt made
the job more difficult, but it preserved the Mediterranean character of the landscape.
Today, in season, the tops of these oaks sway verdantly between the pale gold of the
oats and the intense green of the wheat.

Living quarters for estate workers, with a school for more than forty children,
were built with locally quarried stone in the section known as Piedras Menaras ("Bea-
con Stones"). The importance of religion is emphasized by the chapel's dominant
central position in the ensemble of buildings. Whenever possible, Spanish tradition
requires that a church be dedicated to a family member of its patron, and the chapel
at Piedras Menaras, built in 1940, was named in honor of a great-grandmother of the
Marquess, Santa Micaela del Santísimo Sacramento. It also serves as the mausoleum
of the Casa Valdés family.

The garden was begun in 1945 by Doña Teresa de Ozores y Saavedra, Marchioness of Casa Valdés, a well-known figure in Spanish society, who decided, five

years later, to devote her energies to the study of Spanish gardens, publishing, in 1973, her as-yet-unsurpassed historical monograph. Given Spanish society's customary attitudes, it required strength of character for a woman of her class and generation to become a horticulturist. In much the same way, she made a garden bloom at Piedras Menaras. The conditions were indeed daunting. The terrain is predominantly limestone, which juts up here and there through the thin layer of soil. Rich topsoil was brought in and water was piped from a distant spring; when that was not enough, wells were drilled in the porous chalky rock, to little purpose.

The visitor to Piedras Menaras finds the Marchioness's garden on the left on entering the compound, occupying a level space bordered by her country house, a long, low, red brick building. Access is by means of a flagstone path between masses of lavender bushes that barely let one slip through and two Italian cypresses that seem to form an ogive arch, which is echoed farther on by two Engelman firs *(Abies engelmanii)* that the Marchioness planted in 1960. These herald the long, perfectly maintained lawn that runs between serpentine mixed borders. Antique roses, like the yellow-flowering *Rosa Banksiae "Lutea"*; Japanese jasmine *(Jasminum Mesnyi)*; and wintersweet *(Chimonanthus praecox)* make a great display.

The Marchioness's planting of the variegated *Iris* x *germanica* var. *florentina* combined with even paler hued peonies, musk roses *(R. moschata)*, and Turkestan roses *(R. rugosa)* continues the age-old floral tradition of Spanish flower beds. These species are intermingled in the border next to the terrace with columbine, that strange, delicate flower that could have been created by Hieronymus Bosch. The ground is carpeted with violets and alyssum, and one also finds hollyhocks *(Alcea rosea)*, so typical of a cottage garden. And one cannot but be impressed by the love and patience that have raised a Spanish fir brought from the city of Ronda in Andalucía and a *Juniperus chinensis* var. *Pfitzerana* donated by Princess Piedita de Hohenlohe. Classical sculpture that came by inheritance from the Duchess of Sevillano's old garden in Guadalajara adds a dignified focus to the plantings.

The present Marchioness of Casa Valdés, who inherited Piedras Menaras from her mother and who is also the Countess of Bornos, maintains the garden just as it was left to her, in honor of its creator's memory. With the aid of Bill Tucker, the American horticulturist, in 1986 the Marchioness fulfilled a parental wish by adding a *rosaleda*, in which she can enjoy, from her bedroom window, an outstanding collection of her mother's favorite roses. This new garden, below the terrace on the west side of the house, is densely planted with beds of irises and pansies, which have spread into an even newer woodland garden adjacent to it.

Piedras Menaras: *Rosa Banksiae "Lutea"*

Real Fábrica de Paños

Brihuega
Families: Casado de Arredondo,
Casado González, Hernández
de Rodas, and González Pérez

THE WALLED TOWN of Brihuega is situated in the Alcarria on the steep northern bank of the Río Tajuña that forms the valley bearing its name. In December 1710, when King Philip V (1700–46), the first Bourbon king of Spain, was fighting successfully to secure the throne, a pivotal battle in the War of the Spanish Succession took place here. As a remembrance of the victory and to provide jobs for the king's loyal followers, Philip's son, Ferdinand VI, built a factory for manufacturing cloth for the uniforms of soldiers in the royal armies on a rocky promontory above the town. The Real Fábrica de Paños was not completed until 1783, during the reign of Ferdinand's successor, Charles III.

The factory, a rare surviving monument of eighteenth-century Spanish industrial architecture, was designed by Manuel Villegas and Ventura Padierne, who had worked on the Palacio Real in Madrid. Dominating its numerous storerooms, stables, living quarters, and chapel is the doughnut-shaped, two-story building surrounding a circular courtyard that was constructed to house the twenty looms. Windows in both the outer and inner walls ensured the maximum amount of daylight, extending the workday as much as possible. The southern orientation of the site also improved the light, and not incidentally favored the drying of textiles, which were hung on fixed wooden hangers set outside in rows in a large level space —almost two acres of the three-and-three-quarter-acre site—adjacent to the main building.

The factory fell into disuse in the difficult times caused by the Napoleonic Wars. In 1851, during the period of *Desamortización,* the dissolution of church and crown properties that began in 1835, it was sold at auction to the Cabana family, ancestors of the present-day owners. The new owner's wife later created a garden where the textiles were once set out to dry, from which she might enjoy the panoramic view of the Romanesque church of Santa María de la Peña, the ramparts of Brihuega, and the Tajuña flowing through stands of white poplar, elm, willow, and sumac. The name of the gardener who assisted her is not known. Oral tradition suggests, however, that he was a Frenchman named Veyrat from Grenoble, who, with his son, traveled throughout Spain during the latter part of the nineteenth century, offering their services as garden designers, from a base in Valencia, where they established a nursery to supply their growing business.

In contrast to the imposing circular form of the factory's great ring, the layout of the one-acre garden is determined by a grid of straight paths. Notable are the high arches of Italian cypress that frame them; these remarkable works of horticultural architecture interpret the classical arched colonnade with an undeniably Hispanic inflection. Time, which has augmented the proportions of the hedges, has enhanced the feeling of exaggerated Spanish Romanticism characteristic of the period in which the garden was created. Particularly evocative of this late-nineteenth-century mood are the windmill palms; the wooden birdcages painted green, with their oriental domes covered in zinc; the low circular fountain; the wrought-iron *mirador,* or belvedere, with its commanding view; and the greenhouse adjacent to the southern wall, necessary in the harsh plateau climate. The garden's green silences express a poignant farewell to an era long gone.

OPPOSITE
Real Fábrica de Paños: View of the former
factory, from the north

44

Real Fábrica de Paños: A cypress arch

Real Fábrica de Paños: Ornamental birdcage and windmill palm

T HREE THOUSAND SIX hundred feet above sea level in the province of Soria, Medinaceli is a lofty town perched on a hill overlooking the Río Jalón. It existed before the Romans left their mark in the beautiful form of a famous triumphal triple arch, which is unique in Spain. Of the Arabic presence there remains in the historical record the death here, in 1002, of the great Moorish general Almanzor. The town fell to the Christians in 1124, after which Medinaceli gave its name to the most important duchy of Spanish nobility.

The town has a certain hermetic character owing to the hostile climate, but in the summer flowers in ceramic pots are set out to catch the sun on windowsills and on the streets in front of the houses. Roses, so rooted in Spain and so hardy, predominate, as do the geraniums that disappear with the first frost. There are the red velvety flowers, almost artificial in appearance, of cockscomb *(Celosia cristata),* a species introduced in Europe in the mid-sixteenth century from Central America. The winter cold ends everything except the rosebushes, which are moved against the walls of the houses for warmth, and the cacti and stonecrop plants of the Crassulaceae family that are taken indoors. (The cultivation of such plants in pots throughout the central region of the *meseta* serves as an interesting example of what might be called vernacular horticulture.) Most other plants are kept until mid-autumn, when, in rural areas, they are customarily taken to the cemetery on All Saints' Day (November 1).

Any pot, jar, jug, or crock serves to provide a little life or color. The gardener uses every available container, even tin cans, in his or her desire to increase the number of cuttings: an elderly Spanish gardener used to say that there was no better pot for a plant than an unperforated tin can, so long as one knew how to control the water to sustain the plant.

VERNACULAR GARDEN
Medinaceli

Vernacular Garden, Medinaceli

Los Palacios de Galiana

Toledo
Carmen Marañón de
Fernández–Araoz

THE POETIC MYSTERY of the Palacios de Galiana begins with entangled threads of history and myth that can never be unraveled, for the site will forever be linked to the legends that swirled around the apocryphal exploits of Charlemagne in Spain. One in particular, related in the twelfth-century epic poem *Mainet,* told of how the youthful emperor kidnapped the Moorish King Galafre's daughter, Galiène the Fair, to convert her to the Christian faith and marry her, and of her subsequent death. Legend also had it that King al-Fahri, or Galafre, of Toledo—the son of Yusuf, who in the early eleventh century successfully rebelled against the caliphate of Córdoba, establishing Toledo as an independent kingdom—built two palaces for his daughter, one in Toledo itself, and another, with gardens, along the riverbank. Archaeological research suggests that before becoming a Moorish palace, the structure that was to gather these mythic associations had been a castle of the Visigothic kings of Toledo.

Certainly, the site, near the Alcántara Bridge and across the Río Tajo from the ancient Alcázar, or fortress, of Toledo, has been favored since antiquity. In addition to its proximity to the city and its strategic value, the land, embraced by a bend in the river, is unusually flat; given the richness of the soil and the ease of irrigation, this made it propitious for the cultivation of fruit and other delicacies. The land bordered the Roman road that, by the Middle Ages, led from Toledo to Guadalajara to Saragossa and through the Somport Pass into France: it was called the Gallican or Galiana road.

The Moors held Toledo from 711 to 1085. The high point of their rule occurred during the thirty-two year reign of al-Ma'mun (1043–75), whose court possessed an aura of luxury, culture, refinement, and wisdom. As described by the scholar al-Idrisi (1100–1165), "The gardens surrounding Toledo are furrowed by canals on which mills have been built to irrigate the orchards that produce an abundance of prodigious fruit of an exceptional beauty and taste. Everywhere beautiful domains and well-fortified castles are to be admired."

Such gardens, of course, were not merely functional (or they would not have been gardens), and it is thanks to the imaginative use of water—as a symbol of life, purification, power, pleasure—that another dimension beyond the practical one was evoked by them. We can read, for example, of a crystal and gold pavilion built by al-Ma'mun in the Alcázar; on the roof it had a large reservoir, from which water spilled down the sides into a pool that surrounded it. At night al-Mam'un, lit by torches, would sit within it, so that from the outside the sight formed a marvelous spectacle. Under Al-Ma'mun the fortress by the river became an important royal estate—the Moorish word is *almunia*—with lion fountains filling a pool, as in the palace of Madinat al-Zahira in Córdoba, destroyed in the tenth century, and in the Alhambra in Granada.

It was in 1072, when for a period of nine months al-Ma'mum granted the use of his *almunia* to King Alfonso VI (1030–1109), then temporarily displaced from the throne of León and Castile, that Galiana first came to be known as the Huerta del Rey. From 1077 on, Alfonso, since returned to his throne, began to use the title emperor, for he considered himself king of the Christians, the Muslims, and the Jews. When he attacked Toledo in 1085, he set his tents in the Huerta del Rey that he knew so well and after a long siege conquered the city. In the treaty of surrender, the Arabs agreed to yield the royal Alcázar and the Huerta del Rey with its fortifications in good condition. An edict was published permitting the Muslims to remain in the city; they, however, chose to emigrate to southern al-Andalus rather than live under Christian rule, for, as the scholar Algazel exhorted them, "Enter upon the path of exile, oh, Andalusians, for remaining here is madness. Cloth tends to become frayed at the edges, but the fabric of our peninsula has been torn asunder in the middle."

Los Palacios de Galiana: The *alberca*

Los Palacios de Galiana: Doña Carmen's
house

TOP
Los Palacios de Galiana: Climbing roses on
the side of Doña Carmen's house

Los Palacios de Galiana: The *huerta*;
looking toward the Mudéjar window of
Leonor de Guzmán

Los Palacios de Galiana: The *huerta*;
looking toward the river

The Huerta del Rey remained in royal hands, although it deteriorated over the years, until Alfonso XI (1311–1350) gave it to his mistress Leonor de Guzmán, the mother of the future King Enrique II (1333–1379) of Castile and reputably one of the most beautiful women in the kingdom. The king and his lady had the gardens and palace restored, the latter in the Mudéjar style; the large window that lends such beauty to the main salon was added at this time. It is constructed of four slender black stone columns ending in capitals decorated with the rampant lion of the Guzmán family and carrying three small foliated arches. The property remained in the Guzmán family until the twentieth century, although by the nineteenth century it was virtually abandoned to peasants and gypsies, who used the once-beautiful gardens for pasturage and posed amidst the picturesque ruins of the palace for visiting Romantic painters, among them the British artist David Roberts. The penultimate owner in the Guzmán line was Eugenia María de Montijo, who married Napoleon III of France and became the Empress Eugénie. Toward the end of her life she was possessed by a desire to restore the property, but she died in Madrid in 1920 at the age of ninety-four without realizing her wish. Her heir, the Duke of Peñaranda, sold it to Alejandro Fernández de Araoz in 1959. The new owner did not live long enough to rebuild the Galiana palace, but his widow Carmen Marañón de Fernández-Araoz, the daughter of the distinguished doctor and essayist Gregorio Marañón y Posadillo, has carried out an exemplary reconstruction, employing numerous scholars and architects.

Certainly her noblest and wisest decision was to restore the palace as much as possible but to stop before turning it into a dwelling place; thus the installations required for practical living would not be permitted to efface its medieval poetry. A new "palace," in discreet proximity to the ancient fortress, was built: it is planted with oleander (Nerium Oleander "Album" and "Roseum") and, for color, as they would have appeared in Moorish gardens centuries ago, such flowers as geraniums, pansies, and roses. The focal point of the garden that she created, however, is the medieval palace, and its armature is made up of Italian cypresses that, after thirty years, have attained marvellous height, thanks to the good soil and humid climate they enjoy. Treated with topiary art, the cypresses form figures that are precise, compact, and characterized by elegance, simplicity, and power. Within the palace is a supposed Islamic alberca that in 1960 was covered over with dirt and only recently excavated. It rests in a sunken patio partly surrounded by galleries carried on heavy arches, suggesting that this was once a sunken garden in the Roman or Arab tradition. In this area, a tunnel, presumably a means of escape in time of trouble, leading from the castle to the nearby river was discovered.

The Tajo is a tranquil river before it circles Toledo so dramatically; a river for orchards, fruit, pleasure, ladies: Galiana, Leonor, Eugénie, Carmen. The space between the palace and the river—where a great waterwheel was formerly situated—is once again an orchard and garden. The brick walk that leads from the palace to the footpath beside the river is bordered on both sides by a high hedge of California privet (Ligustrum ovalifolium Hassk), which at one point opens into a small patio with a low, circular white marble fountain of vaguely Arabic inspiration. The huerta around it is a contemporary interpretation of a Koranic paradise: amidst apple, pear, plum, peach, and palm trees, there are lilacs, spireas, and cypresses. Vestiges of the past are in evidence: the arches of an ancient aqueduct; an old Moorish well-curb of terra-cotta; the remains of a clepsydra, or water clock, built by Azarquiel in c. 1060, that were found scattered over a wide area and reassembled here.

What better garden than this exquisite huerta—what in Toledo was called a granadale—could have been made for this medieval palace? In the long stifling afternoons of early summer, cool air rises from the river. Everything shines under the deep, blue Castilian sky, and the only sound is the whistling, rustling, warbling, and billing of the birds. When nothing moves and yet everything pulsates, that is the moment for giving thanks in solitude for so much beauty.

Castillo de Layos

Toledo
Miguel de Oriol e Ybarra
and Inés de Sarriera de Oriol

SCATTERED OVER THE countryside around Roman Toletum (now Toledo) and shaping its subsequent development—in some cases up to the present—were agricultural estates. The *fundus,* or villa, was essentially a farm, producing, at the very least, cereal, olives, and wine (the "Mediterranean triad") and possessing therefore wheat fields, an olive grove, and a vineyard. Cato the Elder (234–149 B.C.) wrote that the ideal rural property ought to include, as well, a garden, a willow grove, an oak grove, and a meadow. Roman villas in Spain influenced the development of the monastery and of the large medieval agricultural estates that acquired different characteristics—and names—in Spain's various regions.

The Romans situated their villas with care, paying special attention to security, the availability of water, and access to roads, qualities that attracted subsequent builders. The fifteenth-century Castillo de Layos was built on the remains of a second-century Roman villa near the Roman road between Metellinum (now Medellín) and Toletum, on ground where even today Roman coins may be unearthed. The

Castillo de Layos: The Mudéjar entrance

OPPOSITE
Castillo de Layos: The *alameda*

54

Castillo de Layos: The pool

imprint of Roman agriculture is still felt in the manner in which the estate is irrigated: water is raised from wells by *norias,* waterwheels turned by donkeys, a technique that was taken over from the Romans by the Moors.

The property was granted by the Catholic Monarchs to their viceroy of Naples, Fernando de Rojas, who built the castle, and it descended over the generations within one extended family until recently. In 1968, Miguel de Oriol, who is one of Spain's leading contemporary architects and whose mother was a member of an old Toledan family with strong ties of affection and tradition to the region, acquired the Castillo de Layos as a country estate and restored it as a family residence. His wife at the time, Carmen de Icaza, preferred to be nearer the center of Spain than were the family properties in the Basque country and Andalucía. The vast estate was to become once again the staging area for great hunts in the Montes de Toledo, and, as in Roman times, there would be both gardens and large tracts of land devoted to cereal production.

The Layos garden, a spiritual marriage of Bilbao and Seville, of mist and light, is the creation of Miguel de Oriol. The fifteenth-century house with its two towers—one square and one round, built on Roman foundations—is set on sloping terrain that rises steeply toward the ten-acre garden in the rear. The exterior of the castle gives the impression of a fortified place, which it indeed once was, and is somewhat forbidding. The main façade facing west is relieved only by a door surmounted by an *ajimez,* or couple-arched window, in the Mudéjar style, with an elaborately ornamented setting of brick and plasterwork. Like many Mediterranean dwellings, the castle turns inward, onto a colonnaded central patio that offers a clear reminiscence of the peristyle and the cloister, with a well that can be relied upon for ice-cold water even in the hottest summer months. Potted hydrangeas have been placed about the rim of the well by Inés de Sarriera, the present lady of the castle. Hers too is the grouping of petunias in beautiful ceramic pots around the old stone basin of the gently murmuring central fountain.

A grassy *alameda,* or walkway, where recently excavated Roman columns have been set at intervals between white poplars, links the forecourt of the castle to the raised ten-acre garden behind it. In the garden façade and on the same axis as the main gate and the front door is a glass projection, like a lantern, designed by Miguel de Oriol, enclosing a Mudéjar ceiling panel rescued from a dilapidated convent in Toledo. From this exceptional *mirador,* the visitor may contemplate the garden with its central swimming pool, or *piscina* as the Romans would have it: a narrow stripe of blue surrounded by granite columns that whisper a suggestion of a peristyle. This Hadrianesque reminiscence of a people who sought to evoke the river Nile in the gardens of ancient Rome is startling on the arid Toledo plateau.

Broad lawns were introduced by de Oriol even though, or perhaps because, they jarred with the tradition and ambience of such a place. Off to the side, a circular path that encloses an olive grove and tennis courts serves for walking horses—as though it were a racetrack or a Roman hippodrome. Such tracks were often found on Roman estates but are rarely preserved in reconstructions; here it appears for the perfectly practical reason that horses are an Andalusian passion of the owner, who raises Arabic and Spanish pure-bred horses.

Layos is a garden of trees, among them the olive and the almond. Shade trees, such as the white poplar, oleaster *(Elaeagnus angustifolia),* blue gum, and the omnipresent Italian cypress, the Roman tree of hospitality, all have a vital role to play in the Manchegan upland in summer.

THE FIRST-TIME visitor to El Castañar who ventures down the long driveway bordered with ancient oaks and elms will be startled to discover at the end of it a turreted mansion in the Scottish baronial style. For this, we have to thank Queen Victoria Eugenia, the British consort of King Alfonso XIII (1902–41), whose taste in country houses was shaped, in part, by her grandmother Queen Victoria's private residence at Balmoral and who wielded considerable influence in the Spanish court. Built in 1909 as the hunting lodge of the Counts of Finat (the Countess was the former Blanca Escrivá de Romaní), El Castañar soon attracted some of the best marksmen in Europe, due to the patronage of the monarchs. The twenty-five-thousand-acre estate, situated in the foothills of the so-called Sierra del Castañar on the edge of the Montes de Toledo and devoted to the growing of grain and the raising of cattle, incongruously retains, near the residence, the typical artisan's cottage where the previous owners had been content to live, along with a Gothic Revival chapel that has more the proportions of a church. On the estate there is a Franciscan monastery that once possessed a famous orchard, watered by stone canals, and that was a favored retreat for its founder, Cardinal Francisco Jiménez de Cisneros (1436–1517), regent during the last years of the reign of Ferdinand el Católico.

El Castañar's seventeen acres of gardens are typical of a landed estate of the *belle époque*. The broad forecourt of the house is occupied by two long, ostentatious parterres *de broderie* bordering the main avenue that are outlined by clipped privet hedges (*Ligustrum japonicum, L. ovalifolium,* and *L. vulgare)* punctuated with topiary cubes of laurel and spheres of boxwood and enclosed by Italian cypresses that were brought by the then very young Count of Mayalde from Granada seventy-five years ago at the behest of his father, the Count of Finat.

The more romantic formal garden to the south of the house, overlooking the mountains on the horizon, is also enclosed by cypresses and has a measured European charm that is heightened by its setting of savage Hispanic beauty. The land slopes downward from the tall rosebushes, so evocative of the fin de siècle, on the terrace next to the house, and the water from the central fountain takes advantage of the incline to cascade merrily down a series of steps into an oval pool bordered by sandy paths. The space is watched over by a classical female statue in marble and there are sculpted horses that still bear scars from the Spanish Civil War. Even though the fighting penetrated this secluded garden, El Castañar's use during the war as a school of political commissars probably saved it from total destruction.

Today the grounds at El Castañar are tended by three gardeners (one of whom has been there more than twenty years) under the eye of the Duchess. The extensive landscape garden beyond the formal areas described would, perhaps, be more impressive if the surrounding countryside were less spectacular in its own right.

EL CASTAÑAR

Toledo
Count of Mayalde and
Duchess of Pastrana

El Castañar: The garden façade

OPPOSITE
El Castañar: The romantic garden viewed
from the house

Santa María de las Nieves

Toledo

Santa María de las Nieves: View of the
main entrance from the olive allée

O**N THE EDGE** of the arid *meseta*, some 1,800 feet above sea level and just six
miles south of the city of Toledo, there existed for several centuries a religious community dedicated to Santa María de las Nieves. Today, one finds
perched on the eastern side of the hill that was once occupied by monks a substantial private residence and, surrounding the eloquent ruins of the ancient monastery,
one of the most inventive of Spain's new gardens to preserve the traditional link
between garden design and spiritual transcendence.

Around 1480, the year of the Catholic Monarchs' establishment of the Inqui-
sition in Castile, Pedro de Rivadeneyra, the prebendary of Toledo Cathedral, which
has been the seat of the primate of Spain since the twelfth century, founded at his
own expense an Augustinian monastery here. In 1494, the prior of Santa María de
las Nieves, as the monastery was henceforth called, came under the authority of the
prior of the Dominican monastery of San Pedro Mártir in Toledo, and in 1531, when
Toledo was not only the capital of Spain but also the hub of empire under Emperor
Charles V, Pope Clement VII founded the Colegio de Santa María de las Nieves with
a chair in theology and arts. The extent of the lands—1,580 acres—is known thanks
to a land registry prepared in the reign of Charles III.

The monastery of Santa María de las Nieves made an important contribution
to Spain's religious and cultural life until the first half of the nineteenth century,
when it was dealt two massive blows from which it never recovered. Napoleon's
troops occupied and pillaged the buildings in August 1809, but far worse was the
Desamortización of 1835, when the government ordered the suppression of the religious orders and the seizure of their lands for subsequent sale at public auction. After
passing through several hands, the property was purchased, in 1945, by the family
of the present owners, who did what they could to preserve the little that remained
of the once-great monastery. While the chants and the chalices that beautified Santa

María de las Nieves have long since departed, that dimension of the past is feeling-
ly recognized in the present organization of the ruined cloister. Here, within the frag-
mented confines of honey-colored cut stone, a lawn, intersected by, appropriately, a
cruciform pattern of paths, is centered on a huge carved stone font. At the four corners laurel trees maintain their vigil, and the only flower permitted to decorate the
broken piers is a rambling white rose, emblem of the Virgin Mary and the source of
that object of Marian devotion, the rosary.

The ambitious building program, whose results can be admired today, was
begun just over ten years ago, under the supervision of the architect Ignacio Vicens
Hualde, who displayed a singular allegience to the project. The work of landscaping
the rocky spur on which the house was built fell to Leandro Silva Delgado, who succeeded in creating here some of his most imaginative garden effects. With characteristic respect for the vegetation that he found in these largely barren hills, Leandro
Silva uprooted from different parts of the property no fewer than thirty-two olive
trees, each one at least one hundred years old, and rerooted them in double rows on
either side of a path leading to the front door of the house. In this sunstruck land,
the twisted trunks support a luxuriant silver grey canopy to shade the pilgrim, and
in their orderly ranks they seem to represent a welcoming community of friars; the
edges of the path beneath their endlessly moving tops are bordered with joyful,
humble English lavender *(Lavandula angustifolia)* that was transplanted from the surrounding hills.

The garden itself cascades down from the southern side of the house in a
series of terraced platforms. Flights of steps, whose descent is marked by the planting, at intervals, of cypress *(Cupressus sempervirens "Stricta"),* lead the visitor to
explore a number of garden rooms carved out of the living rock and only partly visible from the top of the slope. One of the largest of these, a paved patio with a cen-

Santa María de las Nieves: The cloister
garden

ABOVE
Santa María de las Nieves: The water stairs

ABOVE RIGHT
Santa María de las Nieves: Terrace with
pool and roses

tral pool, is enclosed in May with foaming banks of pink roses. Others, more like
monastic cells and planted variously with laurel, rosemary, and the signature lavender, invite contemplation and prayer.

It is fitting that there should be framed in the view out over the rolling
Toledan landscape the hilltop *ermitas* to which the monks once repaired to do
penance in the wilderness. But more eye-catching and representing a no-less-
spiritual quest is the extraordinary water labyrinth that spreads itself at the base of
the hill. In most garden labyrinths, hedges are the means employed to define the
path one must follow without knowing where it leads. The labyrinth at Las Nieves
is different: in its abstraction it lacks hedges or walls as an impediment to vision, and
the channels of water that separate the paths are easily leapt over if one is so
inclined. It is not frightful like the labyrinth of Crete, nor playful, like so many
Baroque ones for pretending to get lost or inciting others to lose their way and making fun of them; it is instead a modern symbol of spiritual questing. The hedging is
reserved for the perimeter; a tight-pressed row of cypresses that blocks out the surrounding landscape so that all attention is concentrated inward. To the contempla-
tive visitor, it is not even apparent whether the primary compositional elements are
the hard, inevitable courses outlined in ceramic tile or the water canals, where the
sky and light are reflected. Indeed, the key to this labyrinth is—as in Zen gardens—
the reconciliation of figure and ground in one vision.

The downward thrust of the garden is felt on the north side of the house as
well, where water cascades down a small channel cut in the center of three flights of
steps into a long, narrow pool that ends at the foot of an ancient stone cross. The
staircase is bordered by double rows of paulownias *(P. tomentosa)* underplanted by
spring-blooming bridal wreath, and the air is perfumed by thyme, lavender, and
rosemary.

OPPOSITE
Santa María de las Nieves: The water
labyrinth

To understand the gardens at La Granja, one must turn one's attention to the time of Philip V, who created them. Fortunately, despite the passage of nearly three centuries, they have remained so clear and beautiful that one could almost be grateful for the losses suffered over time, as elements in a sense really superfluous. In describing La Granja, I do not propose to wear the kind of corrective lenses through which, all too often, this garden has been viewed as a rather inferior imitation of the gardens at Versailles. On the contrary, I have no hesitation in declaring that it is time to recognize La Granja for what it is: a great garden that expresses a uniquely Spanish power.

To be sure, the man who created it was not born king of Spain: he was born French but became Spanish forever. Philip V's grandmother, Maria Theresa of Austria, daughter of Philip IV of Spain, was Princess of Asturias and heir to the Spanish throne before her marriage to Louis XIV of France (1643–1715); his great-grandmother, Anne of Austria, was Louis XIII of France's queen and daughter of Philip III of Spain, who educated the Sun King in the Burgundian protocol of the Spanish court.

For twenty years Philip fought hard to win and keep the Spanish throne for himself and his heirs. Placing himself at the head of an army, the young king crisscrossed his adopted land, in the process getting to know and love it well. Much Spanish blood was shed, and Philip, who frequently suffered hardship and became familiar with defeat, earned the epithet El Animoso ("The Brave"). No doubt, as has often been suggested, the youthful king, who left France at the age of sixteen, never to return, cherished memories of growing up at Versailles. It would indeed not be surprising if, when he came to create his own gardens in Spain, Philip was influenced by the youthful experience of daily exposure to the preeminent French seventeenth-century style that was a hallmark of his grandfather's reign.

What is sometimes overlooked is that at the palace of El Buen Retiro, in Madrid, Philip V took possession of gardens that, in terms of the uses to which they were put, if not in their layout, served as a model for the gardens at Versailles. Maria Theresa of Austria was a young girl at her father's court when Philip IV created El Buen Retiro and she participated in festive occasions that took place in the gardens. Later, at Versailles, she may have been tempted to observe that her father was the first monarch to have been called the Sun King!

But we anticipate the event that was to prove decisive in shaping the king's future course and, at the same time, have a profound impact on the development of a distinctly Spanish style of gardening. In 1719, while pursuing the pleasures of the chase Philip came upon a spot where he decided to build himself a retreat. Here, having abdicated in favor of his son Luis (whose death in 1724 soon returned Philip to power), he would lead a life of retirement from the cares of state. In this regard, La Granja was fundamentally different from Versailles, which was planned and executed by Louis XIV as the showcase of his personal rule.

Fate may be said to have taken a hand in separating the king that day from the rest of the hunt and in guiding him to the Ermita de San Ildefonso, 3,900 feet above sea level in the Sierra de Guadarrama, where he found refuge on the *granja,* or farm, tended by monks of the nearby Monasterio de El Parral. The *ermita,* established in honor of Saint Ildefonso by Henry IV of Castile, was on land subsequently donated to the religious community, in 1477, by the Catholic Monarchs. In resolving to repurchase the property for the crown so that he could realize his dream of building a retreat, Philip, who was nothing if not a devout Christian, committed himself to respect the religious character and purpose of the place that he proposed to take over.

It is no accident, then, that the eye of the visitor to the impressive complex that Philip caused to be raised on this site is caught by the cross that surmounts the central cupola. And the view of the palace from the forecourt is dominated by the Colegiata (Collegiate Church) that, unlike the chapel at Versailles, clearly occupied a preeminent place in the life of the king who built the palace surrounding it. Con-

LA GRANJA DE SAN ILDEFONSO

Segovia
Patrimonio Nacional–Real Casa

OPPOSITE ABOVE
La Granja de San Ildefonso: The garden façade

OPPOSITE BELOW
La Granja de San Ildefonso: The Cascada Nueva

La Granja de San Ildefonso: The Parterre de Andromeda

La Granja de San Ildefonso: An ornamental urn

sistent with the king's wish to respect what had been established on the site, the palace encloses at its heart the Patio de la Fuente, the former cloister of the religious community. In the same way, in laying out the land that the monks had farmed, Philip incorporated their plantings of fruit trees and increased their groves of elm.

In his decision to retire to the mountains north of Madrid, Philip was fully supported by his second consort, the Italian-born Isabella Farnese, a woman of culture and intelligence who gave an early indication of her mettle by dismissing, on the very day of her arrival, the overweening Princesse des Ursins, who had imposed her French taste upon the Spanish court. The influence of the queen can be detected in both the choice of architects commissioned to design the royal residence at La Granja and in the Italianate scale and detailing of the finished building. Isabela was also to make a signal contribution to the laying out of the gardens around the palace, which began at the rear, where the building's façade was, in the fashion of the Baroque, treated with the greatest elaboration. Indeed, history does not record the king's response to the Duc de Saint-Simon who, following a visit to Spain, blasted Philip for breaking so completely at La Granja the rules laid down at Versailles.

To those who argue that the king's seemingly fortuitous selection of site was inappropriate, it may be objected that this was a conscious decision, based on the knowledge that, had he chosen to do so, he could, like his grandfather before him, have projected his power to a seemingly infinite horizon by landscaping the vast Castilian *meseta!* Instead, Philip chose to work within the confines imposed on him by nature, and, in a glorious compromise that intensely irritated the peppery upholder of French standards, permitted an element of wildness to creep into his scheme, which, in Saint-Simon's opinion, was marred by a foreshortening of perspective made inevitable by the encircling peaks.

On paper, the layout of the gardens of La Granja appears to be a conventional pattern of geometric beds and straight paths. In the gardens themselves, this sense

La Granja de San Ildefonso: Apollo

La Granja de San Ildefonso: The Carrera de Caballos

La Granja de San Ildefonso: The Fuente de los Baños de Diana

of rigid order yields, unexpectedly, pleasurably, to the three-dimensional quality of the experience. One finds that, in contradistinction to the orderliness of the plan, there is great freedom in the handling of masses of native and introduced trees and shrubs. The farther up the shoulder of the mountain one explores, the more one loses touch with the discipline displayed in the sunken parterres trimmed with box that frame the palace on both its south and east fronts. The elms of the original monks' grange and the linden and chestnut trees that were later imported from, respectively, the Netherlands and France, give way, harmoniously, to indigenous species, such as Scotch pine *(Pinus sylvestris)* and Pyrenees oak *(Quercus pyrenaica)*, which Philip V's garden architects and plantsmen were content to leave growing in nature.

All told, it is estimated that it took a force of five thousand men working for the space of some twenty years to create the 360-acre garden that we marvel at today. Since it is known that gunpowder was used on occasion to break up rocky outcroppings before paths could be laid and topsoil brought in for the planting of shrubs and hedges, it comes as something of a surprise to find that zones are rarely terraced, and when they are, there is an attempt to integrate the qualities of the terrain.

Had he been more like his grandfather, who spared nothing and no one in subduing the country around Versailles, Philip might well have leveled the small hill that foreshortened the view from the front of the palace and gave him only a limited space in which to lay out the matching pair of lawns with inward sloping floral borders in the forecourt. Because the low hill was on the principal axis occupied by the main gate, the chapel surmounted by a cross, and the sunken parterres, it became the focus of one of Philip's first garden compositions. He scaled the vertical with the

Cascada Nueva, a majestic flight of marble stairs, down which, with the aid of hydraulic wheels, he directed a mighty flow of water that flashed and gleamed its way into the receiving elliptical pool at the base. To complete this garden picture, as always, best seen framed in the second-floor windows of the palace, Philip capped the hill and its central waterfall with an octagonal pavilion decorated with allegories of the four continents where the Spanish monarchy had possessions and crowned by a figure, representing the Triumph of Faith and expressing the Spanish monarch's abiding concerns, that reaches up to the sky.

La Granja de San Ildefonso: The Fuente de Letho

Although the gardens are, at least in the plan, organized around the unifying principal of the main axis, one finds that, in practice, they are composed of two parts, unequal in size and, it has to be said, in the level of interest that they sustain. Everywhere, it seems, a veritable army of animated figures, inspired by Carlo Ripa's *Iconologia,* stands guard. They were carved in marble or cast in lead by sculptors who came from France at royal command, among them Frémin, Thierry, Dumandré, Pitué, and Bousseau. Nothing in a European garden can compare with the Baroque combination of sculpture and water that is the special joy of the gardens at La Granja. And of the twenty-six fountains created, easily the best are concentrated in the smaller of the two sectors of the gardens that lie to the east of the principal axis.

Working under the direction of Aranjuez-based landscape architect Esteban Boutelou and his Spanish associates, to a commission from Queen Isabella, René Frémin and Jean Thierry peopled a succession of pools, popularly known as the Carrera de Caballos, or horses' track, because of the horses that rear their splendid heads from the great basin of the Fuente de Neptuno. Rising, in season, between rows of chestnut trees, tumultuous jets of water advance toward the Pico de Peñalara in a progressively more exhilarating counterpoint of arcing sprays and mythological scenes, each one pregnant with meaning for an audience schooled in the classics. This brilliant ensemble culminates at the top of the range with the Fuente de Andromeda, in which the rich symbolism of Perseus slaying the sea monster sent by the goddess Juno before it could devour the princess chained to an island would not have been lost on loyal subjects of the king. But perhaps the most significant message, "nec sorte nec fato" ("neither chance nor fate"), inscribed on an escutcheon, asserts the rightful place in Spanish history of Spain's first Bourbon king, here depicted as Apollo, a supremely polished lead figure of a man having an enlightened colloquy with Minerva, goddess of wisdom, while the crushed dragon of Ignorance spouts between them, in the most important sculptural group of this entire sequence.

No account of La Granja would be complete that did not mention the historic Fuenta de la Fama, which stands at the far end of the parterre to the south of the palace. Bearing on his back the figure of Fame, who carries one trumpet for proclaiming good and another for evil, the winged horse Pegasus is shown poised for takeoff from the top of Mount Helicon. With a tap of his hoof, so legend has it, Pegasus was able to activate the sacred stream called Hippocrene. Visible in the city of Segovia some seven miles away, the celebrated jet of La Fama, thought to be the highest in Europe, shoots up with volcanic force and, in doing so, seems to energize the already animated figures sprawled on its pyramidal base. The terrace immediately above the Parterre de la Fama ends at the astonishing Baroque wall fountain known as the Fuente de los Baños de Diana, thought to be an artful tribute to another hunter, Philip V, who also paused to refresh himself in an Arcadian setting.

Finally, we cannot leave this area of the garden without at least referring to the Fuente de Letho or Fuente de las Ranas, a marvel of eighteenth-century engineering clothed in the garb of classical mythology. The regal figure of Letho, mother of Apollo and Diana, and also, perhaps, representing Maria Theresa of Austria, the king's Spanish-born grandmother, sits enthroned in a woodland clearing. In the circular basin at her feet, a troop of farmers condemned by the goddess to dwell in the very element that, moments before, they had denied her, hiss and spit as they impotently resist the vividly realized process of transformation from man to frog. The ever-increasing ingenuity and ferocity of the interplay of the jets, whose plumes dash the canopy of protective foliage, is among the most sensational manipulations of water in gardens that rejoice in having the most abundant, varied, and unexpected effects of this magical, life-giving medium to be found anywhere.

Although it may seem like the ultimate in unchanging gardens, La Granja vibrates with the seasons. In springtime it fills with flowers and tender green plants; summer offers its masses of intense green, giving shade against the brightness of the sky; autumn is a refined orgy of color; and there is nothing as elegant as La Granja under snow in winter. No matter the season, the visitor should be sure to see El Mar ("The Sea"). Situated at the opposite end of the gardens from the palace, and buried high up in the enclosing forest, this great artificial lake reflects in the still surface of its cold, pure waters the peaks from which they flow. A place of beauty in its own right, providing solitude and refreshment, El Mar is also, thanks to the elaborate, and largely intact, eighteenth-century system of canals, irrigation channels, pipes and pumps that conduct water to the plants and fountains below, the source of La Granja's seemingly inexhaustible capacity for renewal.

La Granja owes its final form to Italy, the mother of gardens, for its sculptures and fountains; to Spain, a melting pot of gardens, for its magnificent mountain site, for its waters, and for the creative disruption of the rational designs that France, the arranger of gardens, turns out, it sometimes seems, with the dispassionate efficiency of a government committee; and even to England, for a distant echo of the revolutionary garden ideas that can be faintly detected in aspects of its landscaping. At La Granja one finds architecture, geometry, and delicacy at peace with the spirit of liberty and naturalism. In a phrase: beauty in the form of a garden.

THE WESTWARD-FACING Alcázar of Segovia is perched on a great promontory, at the foot of which the Río Clamores joins the Río Eresma. In a lush valley on the north bank of the Río Eresma, in the shadow of the Alcázar on the other side of the river, a small group of houses clusters around a church dedicated to San Marcos, from which this ancient community received its name. It was near here that Leandro Silva Delgado discovered, several years ago, an old millhouse, which he purchased for use as a studio.

What mysterious destiny led an unrepentant wanderer to settle in this particular spot? The landscape architect came here and saw what no one else had perceived, and he patiently amassed what little property he could, thereby making himself the master of an entire historical landscape: behind the house, the ground rises steeply until it becomes a sheer wall of rock, projecting like a canopy, and from this almost Neolithic refuge, the fairy-tale castle—in actuality a Renaissance fortress—appears to fill the sky. By 1976, he had purchased a nearby orchard at the rocky base of the ridge, where springwater gathered in a natural cavity, providing enough to irrigate the land twice a day, even in the dry springtime and the broiling summer. The small plot provided a wonderful creative release to the landscape architect, who is also an engraver, occupied with the patient search for rhythmic harmonies of color and form and inclined to rigor and measure.

EL ROMERAL DE SAN MARCOS

Segovia
Leandro Silva Delgado
and Julia Casaravilla

El Romeral de San Marcos: The garden; looking toward the Alcázar

OPPOSITE
El Romeral de San Marcos: The garden; looking toward the Monasterio de El Parral

75

El Romeral de San Marcos: Stairs leading to the first level of the garden

El Romeral de San Marcos: The upper level

OPPOSITE
El Romeral de San Marcos: Petunias and asters

As an exercise in acquiring self-knowledge, creating one's own garden is an incomparable experience. The garden of Leandro Silva is not an extension of his house but is separated from it by the narrow road that leads to the Monasterio de El Parral higher up the valley to the east. It possesses the exemplary virtue of existing freely, not unlike its peripatetic creator who, even though he makes his home in Spain, continues to travel throughout Europe and Latin America, frequently returning to his native Uruguay.

The garden's principal compositional element is the slender Italian cypress *(Cupressus sempervirens "Stricta")*, sober and deep green in aspect. This species is supported by boxwood *(Buxus sempervirens "Suffruticosa")*, traditionally the essence of Spanish gardening, and rosemary, which gives its name to the garden—*romeral* means "field of rosemary." The lower level of the garden, bordered by the road, is enclosed with a free mixture of English hawthorn *(Crataegus laevigata)* and fire thorn *(Pyracantha coccinea)*. The narrow stairs permitting only one person to pass, the low walls surrounding tiny garden squares, the pots for camellias, and the small *alberca* at the top of the garden, from which water is conducted by means of a narrow, murmuring channel, are all the characteristic warm but discreet hue of terra-cotta.

There are, in Spain, so many green gardens that it is something of a surprise to discover that at El Romeral de San Marcos, the two Castilian seasons—spring with its floral explosion and fall with its almost black greens, reds, and golds—have been planned for with attention to color. Springtime is the most spectacular, when the showy crab apple *(Malus floribunda "Van Houtte")* and the Japanese flowering cherry *(Prunus serrulata)* are decked with colors that will later become fruit, and the narcissus *(N. Tazetta, N. Pseudonarcissus, N. rupicola,* and *N.* x *incomparabilis)* bloom, followed by tulips *(Tulipa Gesnerana, T. humilis,* and *T. Clusiana)* and then peonies and tree peonies. Among unusual species are Santa Barbara redroot *(Ceanothus impressus "Puget Bleu")* and clematis *(C.* x *Jackmanii)*, curiously rare in Spain, that within the scale of blue hues coexists with lavender *(Lavandula angustifolia* and *L. Stoechas)*. With the late-spring flowers bloom antique roses and unusual hybrids that Leandro Silva, inspired by conversations with the late Marchioness of Casa Valdés, collected, among them the now-popular Bourbon rose Souvenir de la Malmaison, hybridized by Beluze in France in 1843; Iceberg, a Floribunda rose hybridized by Kordes in Germany in 1858; The Garland, a Musk rose hybridized by Mills in England in 1835; New Dawn, a Wichuraiana rose hybridized by the Somerset Rose Company in the United States in 1930; and Yvonne Rabier, another Floribunda rose hybridized by Turbot in France in 1910.

Springtime at El Romeral de San Marcos would be incomplete without its Fiesta de los Lirios, a holiday of lilies celebrated every year for the past fifteen by Leandro Silva and his wife, Julia Casaravilla, and their many friends when the irises are also in full bloom. On this occasion, visitors may be reminded of the apostle's saying of lilies that "not even Solomon in all his glory was arrayed like one of these" (Matt., 6:28). Among the irises cared for with loving attention by Jesús and Celestino Martin, the gardeners, are the cultivars Arpège, Baccarat, Deep Space, Etincelle, Siva Siva, Tahiti Sunrise, and Lunar Fire.

Autumn brings the fleeting hues of Norway maple *(Acer platanoides)*, sycamore *(A. pseudoplatanus)*, Montpellier maple *(A. monspessulanum)*, hedge maple that looks like candelabrum, European hornbeam *(Carpinus Betulus)*, English yew *(Taxus bacatta)*, juniper, European beech *(Fagus sylvatica)*, *Parrotia persica*, the elmlike *Zelkova carpinifolia*, witch hazel *(Hamamelis virginiana)*, and myrtle, amidst the evergreen Italian cypress.

Finally, a personal note: the Silvas' terrace in Madrid overlooked the nineteenth-century garden of the Hotel Correcher, the old *palacete* owned by the author's family, in its dying days. They particularly admired the double *Rosa Banksiae "Lutea"* that now drapes with tiny yellow flowers the rocky garden of El Romeral de San Marcos, in which they planted also a tree of heaven *(Ailanthus altissima)* grown from a seed that wafted up to them from that now vanished landmark.

Galicia

Palacio de Oca

La Estrada
Fundación Casa Ducal
de Medinaceli

Palacio de Oca: The upper pond; looking
toward the mill

I N GALICIA, THE landscape is mysterious and still; its gentle rains seem to have erod-
ed the terrain, accounting for its rounded, softened contours, and the dew caress-
es the taut surfaces of leaves that shine in delight. To a surprising extent, this
landscape was shaped by the *pazos,* or manor houses with their gardens and
domains, that for hundreds of years annexed the tracts around them in ever widen-
ing circles. In the same way, they affected social customs, as their well-born owners
provided the provincial milieu with models of behavior.

Insofar as function, form, and name are concerned, the origin of the *pazo* can
be traced to the period of Roman rule. *Pazo* derives from the Latin *palatium,* signifying a palace. Whether the noble families of Galicia exploited their lands directly
or let them out, they tended to plow some of the earnings back into their *pazos,*
which were used as summer residences, and many display the fine craftsmanship of
stonecutters trained in the art for which Santiago de Compostela was famous. Oca,
which was once an estate of almost 25,000 acres, is the only manor house in Galicia called a *palacio* and not a *pazo*; long-held tradition would have it so, and the name
is well merited.

The Palacio de Oca is situated near the town of La Estrada on the southern
slopes of the valley of the Río Ulla, about sixteen miles south of Santiago. Its early

history was shaped by violence: the twelfth-century fortress of Suero de Oca was attacked during his absence by his enemy Alonso de Fonseca, the Archbishop of Santiago, who occupied the property and abducted Suero's wife. The latter died of sadness, and the archbishop retained the manor for himself. It was not until 1564 that Pope Pius V conveyed the abbatial lands to Philip II, who in turn sold them, in 1568, to Doña María de Neira y Vargas. This noble lady's escutcheon, carved in granite at Oca, after the fashion of these great Galician houses, included an heraldic reference to her claim to be a descendant of the mythical Reina Loba, or Wolf Queen, whose son Dario slew a serpent on the banks of the river Arca, otherwise known as Neyra.

The domain of Oca passed by inheritance to the Gayoso family, whose escutcheon shows three trout, cross-joined, on blue stripes; it also appears on Oca's walls. Andrés Gayoso Mendoza married Constanza Arias Ozores, Countess of Amarante, a lady-in-waiting to the queen who, in 1719, received from Philip V the marquisate of San Miguel das Penhas y de la Mota. It was they who, in the early years of the eighteenth century, remodeled the former medieval stronghold, restoring the tower. In the mid-eighteenth century their son Fernando Gayoso Arias ordered the construction of a chapel and a *huerta,* comprising an area of six acres, surrounded by a very high granite wall punctuated by pointed merlons. The remaining land was devoted to the cultivation of cereals and groves of oak and chestnut, species important to the Galician economy.

The granite buildings at Oca—the palace with its tower and the magnificent Baroque chapel that flanks it—form two sides of the plaza into which leads the old royal road that skirts the garden wall. A grove of tall cypresses near the chapel and a large, circular dovecote behind the long, low range of houses for the servants opposite the palace prove the popular proverb, "Capilla, palomar y ciprés, pazo es" ("Chapel, dovecote, and cypress tree, that makes a pazo").

Traversing the main entryway of the palace, one finds oneself in the old service patio, where each day farmers would arrive with firewood and, at harvesttime, their rents in kind. A fountain that was once used to water the farm animals is now the central ornament of a charming garden that was first planted in the second half of the nineteenth century and remodeled in the twentieth. It consists largely of boxwood trimmed in tightly woven, fragrant hedging along with the ball-shaped forms that Bramante had prescribed for gardens since the Renaissance, forms that not incidentally echo the fountain's rounded finial.

Here, the observant visitor may perceive on the wall below the eaves at one end of the house a carved hand with pointing finger accompanied by the word *prosiga* ("continue") and the date 1746, evidence that the ambitious building program commenced in the early years of the eighteenth century was never completed. Even without this projected wing, Oca is magnificent enough, and has had the good fortune of having been cared for in recent years with singular devotion and understanding. Whoever passes through the doorway under an arch in the south wall of the patio enters a dazzling garden. The basis for this enlightened conservation policy carried out by the Duke of Segorbe, whose mother, the Duchess of Medinaceli, inherited the property in 1947, is to be found in the Archivo Medinaceli in the Casa de Pilatos in Seville, one of the richest collections of documents pertaining to Spanish palaces.

To fully appreciate the garden at Oca, one must first come to grips with a paradox. The climate of Galicia is such that irrigation is not generally an overriding concern of gardeners and farmers, but one associates Oca with water treated reverentially, though without vain display, as it is in other parts of Spain where it is indeed a scarce resource. The main undertakings carried out in the garden in the eighteenth century were focused on the construction of canals and ponds, for both practical and aesthetic purposes. A stream called the Oca ó Mauro enters the walled enclosure on the high ground to the east (a secondary conduit sends water via a stone canal to the cultivated fields), where it becomes a stone canal that flows in the direction of the palace. The water first enters a great stone basin sheltered by a roofed

Palacio de Oca: The dam between the ponds, with a conduit in the form of a serpent

Palacio de Oca: Stone benches at the end of the linden avenue

structure open on four sides called a *lavadero,* in which the yarn used for weaving could be washed and dried, and flows from there into the first of two 150-foot-long, narrow *estanques,* one below the other, of surpassing beauty, that are set at an angle to the south front of the palace and extend almost the full width of the walled enclosure. These ponds, dating in their present form from the early eighteenth century, disrupt what would otherwise be a relatively conventional garden design: the avenue of large-leaved lindens that begins at the Puerta del Bosque, the forest gate in the south wall, providing the garden with its main axis aligned on the archway leading to the patio of the palace, and that one might expect to extend all the way to the palace, terminates at the ponds.

The dam between these two ponds fulfilled a double purpose: it provided the power for a gristmill that was moved later in the century to the head of the first pond, where it can still be found, and a walkway along the top of it permitted passage over the water from one side to the other. This elegant bridge's inward-facing benches invite the visitor to rest under a pergola of grapevines that has only recently been restored. Water from the upper pond flows through the carved head of a serpent into a circular stone bowl on a pedestal, from which it overflows into the lower pond in an unnecessarily refined but beautiful display. Estate records reveal that Esteban Ferreiro of Santiago contracted on October 12, 1717, to complete work on the bas-relief sculpture of the stone figure of the giant that holds the serpent—a reference to the de Neira family crest—before 1720. It was probably Ferreiro too who created the famous stone boat carrying a master and his servant that appears to float placidly in the lower pond. This island-boat was once planted with espaliered orange trees, for which its orientation provided—in an admittedly capricious manner—the greatest exposure to the sun. That the boaters are fishing in the still, reflecting waters suggests that in these pools fish—perhaps they were trout—were formerly raised for food as well as for diversion.

The *huerta,* with its straight paths covered with grapevines on wooden pergolas—now being restored—to shelter the constant passage of carts and men going to and from the palace, provided superb harvests of fruits and vegetables. Following the medieval monastic tradition the kitchen garden was bordered with herbs and simples and provided the palace with navicula, beans, string peas, purple broccoli, artichokes, cardoon, cabbage, escarole, peppers, potatoes, asparagus, and strawberries. The mostly espaliered fruit trees in the orchard bore pears, apricots, cherries, plums, passion fruit, and, primarily, oranges, for Galicia was the major exporter of oranges to England in the eighteenth century. There were also lemon trees that were covered over in winter with mats made from maize.

All was not arranged for practical use alone. Everything in stone—walls, staircases, balustrades, pergolas—possessed the Baroque baronial character that is the signature of the Santiago stonemason. We know that there were flowers, for example, clematis *(C. Flammula),* in some of the square beds, and from 1789 on, there were "young trees from Leirado," in all probability camellias imported from Portugal, one of the places from which the soon-to-be-fashionable flowers entered Europe; these the administrator of the estate was at first unable to name because of their novelty. Since 1799 there have been tulips, the floral passion of the eighteenth-century.

The horticultural revolution originating in England in the eighteenth century reached Oca a century later, occasioning the transformation of the geometrically laid out *huerta* into a garden of somewhat curvilinear design. This task was entrusted in 1845 to François Vié, the head gardener of the Palacio Real in Madrid, who planted exotic species of great size that provided shade but endangered the fruit trees and vegetable plants. These were no longer so essential anyway, for the owners now remained almost all year long in Madrid. Gardeners brought in eucalyptus, cryptomeria, and tulip trees and combined them with indigenous plants like yew and strawberry trees; they also added plots of grass, rose arbors, hortensias, and calla lilies. Today, in the ongoing restoration of the gardens, the exquisite, palatial accent of the orchard is once again being highlighted.

OPPOSITE ABOVE
Palacio de Oca: The master of stone boat

OPPOSITE BELOW
Palacio de Oca: Merlons and spheres along the wall enclosing the lower pond

La Saleta: The chapel with bottlebush in the foreground

La Saleta: The patio of the old *pazo*

THE CLIMATE OF the Rías Bajas, on the west coast of Galicia, is a gardener's paradise. In winter, with a median temperature of 57 degrees, frosts are rare; summers have few days hotter than 80 degrees; and there is an annual rainfall of seventy-one inches. What experienced gardener does not dream of such conditions?

One who did was Robert Gimson of Leicester, England, who, after spending several summers on vacation in Galicia with his wife, Margaret, and their children, decided to live his dream. La Saleta, the five-acre property they purchased in 1968, consisted of a granite courtyard house and a separate chapel situated beneath a sheltering grove of eucalyptus on a hillside sloping gently toward the east. The property had been abandoned four years earlier following the death of the last descendant of Mateo Pérez de Caamaño of Cambados, who built the house in 1721.

In 1870, one Severo Pérez Cardecid built the chapel, which became a popular pilgrimage site because of its dedication to the Virgin of La Saleta, the name in Spanish of La Salette, the mountainous spot near Grenoble where the Virgin Mary was said to have appeared to two village children. Severo Pérez, who attained the rank of lieutenant colonel in the service of Queen Isabella II, had inherited the estate from his grandfather, Don Mateo. The name La Saleta fits the smallest *pazo* in Galicia perfectly, because *saleta* or *salita* is Spanish for "small room." A land survey by the Marquess of La Ensenada in 1752 recorded that on this site there was a farm of about ten acres, with a house and an oak grove, and a hamlet of twelve dwellings named Sobreira, the local term for cork oak, of which there are specimens in the present garden.

The basic layout of the garden was achieved quite quickly, once it had been

decided to construct a more modern house on the shoulder of the hill near the old house and the chapel. The slope below it was terraced with a series of stone landings and stairs, known as Robert's folly, that was never actually completed; it is centered on a rectangular pond for aquatic plants that has been taken over by frogs. Gimson was impatient to begin planting species from far-off places and studying their development. Many of these were introduced into the woodland area that forms the eastern boundary of the property. Here, he planted cluster pine to provide a sheltered zone for tender plants. Rhododendrons, of which the yunnan rhododendron *(Rhododendron yunnanense "Damozel" and "Bow Bells")* is the most notable, were also brought in.

The plants most eagerly sought after by Robert Gimson originated in Australia and South Africa, although these did not adapt as well to the fairly exposed sandy slope in which he planted them as those from New Zealand and other Pacific islands. Examples of the former include the kangaroo-paw *(Anigozanthos flavidus)*, with its everlasting green leaves; the bottlebush *(Callistemon linearis)* and the crimson bottlebush *(C. citrinus "Splendens")*; Australian pine *(Casuarina verticillata, C. stricta, C. torulosa,* and *C. tunuissima)*, of rapid growth; banksia *(Banksia collina* and *B. grandis)*; waratah *(Telopea speciosissima)*; protea *(P. grandiceps, P. longiflora,* and *P. compacta)*; and acacia, known as wattles in Australia *(A. cultriformis* and *A. longifolia)*. Especially beautiful among the acacias are wirilda *(A. retinodes "Floribunda")*, which flowers in all four seasons, and the surprising gold-dust acacia *(A. acinacea)* of gorgeous flowering during the month of August.

There are many examples of plants from North and South America, like gaura *(G. Lindheimeri)*, a shrub with white flowers from the American South and northern Mexico that looks like an explosion of fireworks; franklinia *(F. Alatamaha)*, with extremely beautiful white flowers similar to camellias, from the state of Georgia in the United States; climbing Chilean bellflower *(Lapageria rosea)*, which owes its name to its dazzling pink-purple bell-shaped flowers; and nasturtiums *(Tropaeolum majus)* from Brazil and Peru, known popularly as *capuchina*.

Beneath the pines and out in the open there is now a veritable forest of camellias. The three specimens of *Camellia saluanensis* planted when the property was just purchased have grown to a height of twelve feet. According to Robert Gimson's notes, he planted varieties of *Camellia Pitardii, C. miyagii, C. oleifera, C. kissi, C. irrawadiensis* and *C. hongkongensis,* as well as tea plants *(C. sinensis)*.

Robert Gimson was a conscientious English gardener. He corresponded with botanical gardens, nursery owners, and seed collectors around the world and was a frequent visitor to flower shows, especially the traveling Camellia Fair, in which, in 1985, he won the Golden Camellia Prize. A tall, imposing man, he was always accompanied by his wife, Margaret. Until his death in 1987, Gimson dedicated himself to amassing a collection of rare plants that had not been cultivated before in Spain. If there are larger gardens with more species in Spain—the botanical garden at Marimurtra comes to mind—there are none in which one man, often working alone and on a restricted budget, has achieved so much.

Following Robert Gimson's death, his widow Margaret, a woman of great courage, recognizing the importance of her late husband's work, decided to preserve the garden, even though she had never cared much for it. Despite the destruction wrought by Hurricane Hortense and the loss of several species, the garden appears more beautiful now than ever. Its owner confesses: "A woman's touch." It is fascinating and instructive to see the sixteen card catalogues, filled with thousands of index cards minutely detailing the origin, planting, maintenance, location, number, seeding, and—if it did not survive—the death of each plant. These have been maintained since the garden's inception and are now preserved, along with plans giving the location of individual plants. This is the foundation upon which the lady of the house continues to build, with the assistance of one full-time and one part-time gardener. La Saleta is an asset Galicia can ill afford to lose, because in this corner of Spain loving hands have caused to take root a wealth of species from around the world.

OPPOSITE ABOVE
La Saleta: The woodland garden

OPPOSITE BELOW
La Saleta: "Robert's folly"

ᴀᴛ ᴛʜᴇ ᴍᴏɴᴀsᴛᴇʀɪᴏ de San Lorenzo de Trasouto there still exist vestiges of the *ermita* founded in 1216, during the reign of King Alfonso IX of León (1188–1230), by Martín Arias, Bishop of Zamora, who was born in Santiago, as Santiago de Compostela is known throughout Spain. In the fifteenth century the monastery became the property of the Counts of Altamira, under whose patronage it was ceded to the Franciscan order. The patrons had the right to name abbots and to maintain for themselves rooms for spiritual retreat, a custom initiated by the royal court and adopted by the grandees of Spain. The Cuarto de los Condes ("Chamber of the Counts") had the distinction of being occupied by Emperor Charles V, who went on retreat here during Lent in the year 1520. The monastery was appropriated by the state during the period of *Desamortización* in the nineteenth century and restored to the Altamira family only as a result of a lawsuit brought by the Duchess of Medina de Las Torres, a great-grandmother of the present owner.

The monastery's cloister is a marvel, on account of the topiary art of its four-hundred-year-old trimmed boxwood. The great square space, with corners at the four cardinal points, has two levels. The upper gallery's arcades have been glazed, creating a spacious corridor that is comfortably furnished and well lit. The lower gallery has not been enclosed; it is a space for recreation on the hottest days, as it is lined with hundreds of plants and shaded by vines that cling to the slender columns, crowning the arches with greenery.

As in the Patio de los Evangelistas at the Escorial, the layout compartmentalizes the space into quadrants by means of two broad paths that intersect in the center and by the further subdivision of the quadrants with crossing paths. All of the resulting squares are filled with boxwood hedging—1,080 square feet of it—except for two on the southeast side, where there is a sunken pool with a fountain presided over by a fifteenth-century stone statue of the Virgin. Even with regular trimming, the five-foot-tall hedges have filled out so much that the gardener in charge of maintaining this remarkable example of topiary art can barely squeeze between the walls of brilliant green twice a year to clip them; he performs the miracle of preserving the original designs. We can recognize among the symbols of the faith described by the hedging the pilgrim's shell of Saint James, the Alpha and the Omega, the initials JHS, and the crosses of Saint Dominic and of the Order of Calatrava.

Cʟᴏɪsᴛᴇʀ Gᴀʀᴅᴇɴ,
Mᴏɴᴀsᴛᴇʀɪᴏ ᴅᴇ Sᴀɴ
Lᴏʀᴇɴᴢᴏ ᴅᴇ Tʀᴀsᴏᴜᴛᴏ

Santiago de Compostela
Duke and Duchess of Medina
de Las Torres and of Soma

ᴏᴘᴘᴏsɪᴛᴇ
Cloister Garden, Monasterio de San
Lorenzo de Trasouto

Pazo de Ortigueira

La Coruña
Marquess and Marchioness of
Santa Cruz de Rivadulla

A T THE END of the Middle Ages, the Galician nobility began to return to the
agrarian traditions of the Roman period, taking advantage of the hospitable
soil and climate as well as the labor of their subjects, who were truly devoted to the land. By the late fifteenth century, the Torre de Ortigueira, a medieval
defensive tower named for the stinging nettle that grows throughout northern Spain
and overlooking the Río Ulla near the town of Vedra, was also known as the Granja
de Ortigueira. The *casa fuerte,* or fortified house, was acquired, in 1520, by the Mondragón family, who enlarged it and added muted Renaissance accents, making it the
nucleus of a typical Galician *pazo.* The severe granite house has partly whitewashed
walls on which the Mondragón family coat-of-arms is prominently carved. In the
forecourt, a fountain that has been fed by an underground stream since the fifteenth
century carries an ornate Baroque frame contributed by a master stonemason from
Santiago in 1673 that displays the arms of Andrés Ibáñez de Mondragón, created
Marquess of Santa Cruz de Rivadulla in 1683, this being virtually the only conces-
sion that the practical ensemble makes to art.

The seventy-four-acre estate commands, from within its three-and-a-half-
mile perimeter wall, a broad expanse of the rich, fertile valley of the Río Ulla, dominated by the Pico Sacro, or Holy Mountain. According to records dating back to

Pazo de Ortigueira: The olive allée

1425, it originally produced flax, sugarcane, and wheat, but in the seventeenth and eighteenth centuries Galicia revitalized its agricultural production with two American species: corn and potato. From the sixteenth century there remains an unusual allée of olive trees, probably the northernmost in Galicia, a reminiscence of their intense cultivation in antiquity, especially in the area of the Río Miño to the east. In the late twentieth century, the land produces fruit, wine, and milk.

The garden proper covers five acres. In the upper part, a regular plan is apparent but has not been absolutely imposed upon the terraced terrain, and the ancient custom of covering the paths with pergolas supporting grapevines is maintained. There is a recollection of the traditional *huerto* here, for it was an apple orchard until the nineteenth century. Farther away from the house, around a steep declivity, within what was called, in the Spanish gardening tradition of courtly inspiration, the *reservado,* was made a woodland garden where indigenous plants intermingled with others that were introduced. Here one finds a *cascada* that looks natural but was created in the fifteenth century when the stream that had hollowed out the valley before joining the Río Ulla was dammed in several places to make pools intended for the breeding of fish. This, like the *huerto,* is a centuries-old custom of Spanish monasteries and royal residences. As the water overflows the low walls it forms a tiered waterfall that empties into a paved irrigation canal. Near the falls, one finds such typical Galician species as English oak, English walnut, and Spanish chestnut, along with European filbert, European beech, smooth-leaf elm, boxwood, European white birch, and naturalized camellias. Nearby there is a stone bench and table where Gaspar Melchor de Jovellanos (1744–1811), the leading figure of the Spanish Enlightenment and a frequent guest at Ortigueira, spent much time in shaded meditation.

On the highest terrace above the *cascada,* there is a large, granite-lined *estanque* that provided water for three sixteenth-century stone gristmills, last restored in 1767 but no longer in use, whose rural Baroque spirit partakes equally of courtliness and provincialism. Tiny granite benches with cushions of velvety moss placed at a later date beside the reservoir invite contemplation of the reflections in its waters of two spectacular tulip trees, planted in 1850, and now, reputedly, the largest in Europe. Near the pool are two intriguing additions of, respectively, the seventeenth and eighteenth centuries: the so-called Carrera de Bojes, a tunnel of greenish light formed by the interconnecting branches of twelve-foot-tall boxwood; and a spherical stone clock, a product of the Age of Enlightenment, which was originally connected to a tiny cannon. When, at the appropriate hour, sunlight, refracted through a magnifying glass, lit the fuse, the cannon would fire and everyone on the estate knew that it was time to start, or stop, their appointed rounds.

The writer who, in 1875, described Ortigueira as an *"oceano de maravillas,"* was impressed by the *pazo's* groves of orange and lemon trees, and also by the many exotic species growing there. Ortigueira's long-established reputation as a garden of rare plants may be said to have originated with Juan Ignacio Armada y Mondragón, the third Marquess of Santa Cruz de Rivadulla, in the late eighteenth century. This keen student of botany traveled throughout the New World, collecting many of the plants that are today the garden's greatest glories. From America came giant sequoias, although they exist now only in an old photograph, and a double row of southern magnolias. Of the fourteen venerable survivors, two stand out: one is the support for a climbing thorny oleaster *(Elaeagnus pungens)* that is unique in Europe because of its size. The other is a magnolia tree almost five yards in circumference, judged to be the largest known. Possibly one can attribute to this period as well the first camellias of the soon-to-be-unequaled collection, and the garden's magnificent specimen of pokeweed *(Phytolacca dioica),* commonly known as *ombú* in its native Argentina, that is unique in Galicia. The garden began to acquire an eclectic aspect—between Neoclassical and Romantic, though without the loss of classical forms—that was typical of the age of Romanticism in Spain.

Iván Armada y Fernández de Córdoba, who owned the *pazo* between 1880 and 1899, was the next serious gardener at Ortigueira, and he worked with a French gardener whose name is not recorded. Uncle Ivan, as the seventh Marquess was always known, had received a polished education in England and possessed a cultured spirit. A decidedly nineteenth-century area, close to the house, shows the stamp of his sensibilities: Two ninety-foot thread palms guard the edge of a circular pool, surrounded by gunneras *(G. manicata)* first planted in 1888. He also introduced here Harrington plum yew *(Cephalotaxus Harringtonia),* Tasmanian tree fern *(Dicksonia antarctica),* crape myrtle, and Cape jasmine *(Gardenia jasminoides).* Near the pool he constructed a greenhouse whose terraced interior permits balanced sunlight to reach the plants sheltered there. His most notable contribution, however, may well be the product of his passionate enthusiasm for the camellia, of which it is estimated that he amassed some three hundred varieties. Alfonso Armada y Comyn, the present Marquess, and his son Juan Armada y Diez de Rivera, an agronomist, maintain an ensemble of more than two hundred varieties that constitutes, for many garden visitors, Ortigueira's greatest attraction. Camellias, which bloom from October to May, are a heaven-sent gift in Galicia. The dignified grey stone of Galician architecture and the shiny deep greens of the indigenous vegetation are the perfect background for these limpid, delicate, and at times dramatic flowers that light up even the rainiest winter day and penetrate the Galician mists.

Pazo de Ortigueira: The Baroque fountain

Pazo de Ortigueira: A courtyard with pampas grass

Pazo de Ortigueira: The *estanque* with tulip trees

Pazo de Ortigueira: Thread palms beside
the circular pool

Pazo de Ortigueira: Uncle Ivan's
greenhouse

OPPOSITE
Pazo de Ortigueira: The woodland garden

Catalonia

Cloister Garden, Monasterio de Poblet

Vimbodí
Religious congregation

Cloister Garden, Monasterio de Poblet:
View from the cloister

Ramón Berenguer IV (1137–1162), king of Aragón and Count of Barcelona, founded the monastery of Poblet, about fifty-five miles west of Barcelona, in 1149, on a spot near the Francolí River known as Populetum because of the presence of white poplars and brought in monks from Fontfroide, near Narbonne. The monastery's structure follows the Cistercian plan, which rejected architectural ornamentation as superfluous, the emphasis of the order being placed upon asceticism and charity. The bare style is related to the Romanesque, but has, in its absolute simplicity, a grandeur all its own. The church and one of the cloister's galleries follow the Cistercian model; later, under King Jaime I (1213–76), the Gothic pointed arch was introduced to Poblet and the cloister was completed in this style.

Poblet is one of the supreme examples of a medieval Spanish royal residence adjoined to a monastery protected by the monarch. Like a medieval walled town, it is surrounded by ramparts to ensure his security. Here the king found refuge during his frequent campaigns, and here, if he died elsewhere, he would be returned for burial. Among the other precursors of the Escorial are Santa María la Real (1032) in the kingdom of Navarre; Las Huelgas Reales (1180) in Castile; and San Juan de la Peña (before 858), used by the kings of Aragón until the reign of Ramón Berenguer IV, who also founded Santas Creus (1158) for this purpose. The first king of Aragón to be buried in Poblet was Jaime I, the conqueror of Majorca and grandson of the founder, and until the fifteenth century almost all of the rulers of Aragón were

interred here. Among the great protectors of Poblet were the dukes of Segorbe and Cardona.

The cloister was the center of Spanish monastic life. The earth enclosed by it had various uses, from a burial ground to a *huerto*. Given Poblet's scale, with ample land for food crops outside the monastery, a garden of medicinal and aromatic herbs, or simples, would have been more in line with the immediate needs of the monks. In the reign of Ramón Berenguer IV, quite extensive botanical knowledge was collected at the court of Aragón, some of it translated from Arabic and Jewish sources into Catalán. As in almost all medieval monasteries, the cloister at Poblet offered a sheltered passage between the chapter house, the refectory, and the kitchens. The library, formerly the scriptorium, was also next to the cloister. Intruding into the cloister garden from the twelfth-century refectory and contemporary with it is a domed hexagonal pavilion supported by Romanesque arches carried on columns. Diamond-shaped openings in the arches unexpectedly light the interior, which contains a stone fountain for the monks' ablutions, as required by the rules of the order.

Following the *Desamortización* in 1835, Poblet was pillaged by mobs from the surrounding countryside. Only in the 1940s was the fabric restored and the Cistercian community reestablished. It is hoped that the present planting of the cloister will one day be replaced with an authentic reconstruction based on historical research. Poblet was declared a National Monument on July 13, 1921.

Cloister Garden, Monasterio de Poblet:
The fountain

B ARCELONA'S ATMOSPHERIC BARRI Gòtic, or Gothic quarter, is a labyrinth of narrow medieval streets close to the city's harbor that was sharply bisected by the modern Via Laietana in the late nineteenth century. In 1926, Catalán financier, politician, and art collector Francisco Cambó moved into the top two floors of a ten-story Art Deco office building that he constructed on the avenue. Cambó at that time was preparing for the famous International Exposition in Barcelona in 1929, for which he had been named general director. To design the duplex he chose the young architect Adolfo Florensia, who followed Cambó's ideas closely.

When a man like Cambó, whose paintings today comprise important parts of museum collections in Barcelona and Madrid, wants to build a house in which to enjoy his art, he is able to get exactly what he wants: a private residence in the crowded commercial heart of the city, perched above Gothic towers and belfries, with vistas of the sea from extensive gardens.

The landscape architect Jean-Claude-Nicholas Forestier, who, working closely with Cambó, had been in charge of remodeling Barcelona's Montjuic Park for the exposition, was asked to make a rough plan of a garden for his colleague's future home. But that was the extent of his participation. In final form, it was a fully realized garden on two levels, distinguished by the presence of specimen trees, such as mulberry, willow, palm, and cypress; cypress hedges; walls covered with ivy and bougainvillea; paths of fine gravel edged by seasonal flowering plants; tiled patios; lawns; fountains; a pavilion; and two pools.

The entrance to the Guardans residence is on the ninth floor. On this level, the garden curves around two sides of the building, forming an L. The north side is the favorite spot of Elena Cambó (the daughter of Francisco Cambó) and Ramón Guardans. There is a pool with a table and chairs in the shade of white mulberry (*Morus alba*) and Seville orange trees, and in the summer one can feel the sea breeze in the only private garden in downtown Barcelona to enjoy it. On the east side the view to the sea includes the Gothic tower of the beautiful church of Santa María del Mar. Conscious of the visual impact of a nearby building, Cambó had the painter Sunyent cover its enormous surface with murals of sailing ships in sepia and white, illustrating Barcelona's great maritime heritage.

A narrow staircase whose entrance is almost completely hidden by English ivy (*Hedera Helix*) leads to the garden's upper level, where the children of the family play and dance parties are held beside a small pavilion of Carrara marble brought by Cambó from Italy. In summer this glorious structure is covered by a thick layer of Virginia creeper (*Parthenocissus quinquefolia*) that enhances the unexpected pleasure of being serenaded by the carillon of the neighboring cathedral. Beside the pavilion, presided over by an elegant sculpted swan and inset in a manicured lawn, is a remarkable oval pool framed with delicate terra-cotta tiles. The bottom, constructed of glass brick, also functions as a skylight for the music room below, a magical space filled with light filtered by the undulating water.

Underlying the garden are concrete funnels that resemble enormous flowerpots and that flow into a central drain. Layers of cross-joined roof tiles were set down, on top of which was placed first a layer of large pebbles and gravel and then a layer of soil three feet deep. In this way, plants—some more than fifteen feet tall—were able to anchor their roots. Despite the wind, nothing has ever been uprooted, and during the half century since the garden was built, there have been no cracks or leaks.

Francisco Cambó lived in this house from 1926 until 1937, and in his *Memorias* he correctly predicted that the house would be famous for its garden.

CAMBÓ RESIDENCE

Barcelona
Ramón Guardans and
Elena Cambó

OPPOSITE
Cambó Residence: The lower level, with a view of Montjuic in the distance

Cambó Residence: The lower level

Cambó Residence: The lower level, with murals by Sunyent in the background

OPPOSITE ABOVE
Cambó Residence: The pavilion on the upper level and the cathedral

OPPOSITE BELOW
Cambó Residence: The pool on the upper level

Hortus Botanicus Marimurtra

Blanes
Fundación Carlos Faust

THE NAME MARIMURTRA pays tribute, in Catalán, to the Mediterranean Sea *(Mare Nostrum)* and the myrtle tree *(Myrtus communis)*; both are incorporated in the insignia of the Marimurtra Botanical Garden, known more formally as the Estación Internacional de Biología Mediterránea. Marimurtra was established by Carlos Faust (1874–1952), a German whose business brought him to this beautiful stretch of Catalonia's Costa Brava. Beginning in 1921, he dedicated himself to the creation of a scientific garden, on land that he gradually acquired in the vicinity of the town of Blanes.

The rugged coastal site reaches from Monte San Juan to the sea, and fully two-thirds of it, not open to the public, is devoted to preserving the indigenous species that Faust discovered in the long-cultivated vineyards on the property. Among them are such typical Mediterranean flora as oak, pine, arar, juniper, mastic, broom, rosemary, boxwood, buckthorn, myrtle, rockrose, heath, heather, and European fan palm. Thus the one-third of the garden devoted to regional flora and cactus, to which the public is admitted, is situated at the heart of a thirty-seven-acre estate that preserves the essential character of the Mediterranean maquis.

Faust collected exotic species from the most diverse latitudes, most notably cacti and succulents, which are grouped in two rock gardens: those from South Africa and those from South America. There are torch cactus *(Trichocereus Spachianus)*, maguey *(Agave americana)*, sisal hemp *(A. sisalana)*, old man cactus *(Cephalocereus senilis)* of great height, as well as such spine cacti as barrel cactus *(Echinocactus Grusoni)*, large barrel cactus *(E. ingens)*, and organ pipe cactus *(Lemaireocereus Thurberi)*. Particularly dazzling are the flowers of the ice plant *(Mesembryanthemum)*. Among the subtropical plants is an impressive collection of palms, among them date palm, Canary Island date palm, Senegal date palm *(Phoenix reclinata)*, jelly palm *(Butia capitata)*, Chilean wine palm *(Jubaea chilensis)*, with its curved yellow flowers hanging spectacularly to the ground, and thread palm, whose dry leaves, which are indiscriminately removed in other gardens, are wisely left on the trunks to protect them from the excessive summer heat. The araucarias include Norfolk Island pine *(A. heterophylla)*, Chilean pine *(A. araucana)*, and bunya-bunya pine *(A. Bidwillii)*, which were planted in 1924 along with a eucalyptus collection. An area of the garden provides demonstrations of the Mendelian laws of inheritance and examples of morphological convergence among plants, and includes collections of toxic, medicinal, and aromatic plants. On the slopes nearest the sea are the collections of regional flora from every continent. An old quarry has been converted into a pool for aquatic species: water lilies, lotus, hyacinth, and calla lilies, accompanied by graceful papyrus.

If Marimurtra is a garden intended for study and research, its founder knew also how to give it an aesthetic dimension. The layout respects the topography of the garden's cliff-top site, while the planting has been ordered in harmony with science: it has the character of a Mediterranean garden in which one just happens to find flora of the whole world. Marimurtra's architectural elements—pergolas, pool, staircases—were determined primarily by practical needs. The one exception is the classical pavilion overlooking the sea at the end of one of the prettiest garden stairs in Spain. The pavilion Faust dedicated to Carolus Linnaeus, the father of botany; the stairs bear the name of Dr. P. Font y Quer, Faust's friend and counselor and a famed botanist in his own right.

Since Faust's death, the foundation has continued to catalogue, cultivate, and study plants found in restricted ranges—many of which are threatened by extinction. Among its activities is the publication of an *Index Seminorum* to facilitate the exchange of seeds among botanical gardens. Two administrators and eight gardeners are responsible for maintaining a total of 4,000 species. Visitors to the Costa Brava who may be tempted to bypass Blanes in favor of the Cape Roig Botanical Gardens near Callela, another *jardín de aclimatación,* are strongly advised that they should on no account miss Marimurtra.

OPPOSITE
Hortus Botanicus Marimurtra

Hortus Botanicus Marimurtra: The pool,
planted with aquatic species

OPPOSITE ABOVE
Hortus Botanicus Marimurtra: The cactus
garden, with the cypress walk in the
background

OPPOSITE BELOW
Hortus Botanicus Marimurtra: The cactus
garden

Hortus Botanicus Marimurtra: The
Linnaeus pavilion at the foot of the main
stairs

No matter how many extraordinary gardens the sensitive and impressionable visitor may know, the garden at Santa Clotilde is sure to be an overwhelming experience. And not alone on account of the landscape, one of the most beautiful in all Spain. Situated on a rocky promontory from which steep paths lead down to the coves of Los Fanales and Santa Catalina, the house was built by the late Marquess of Roviralta in the 1920s on the then undiscovered Costa Brava. In the amphitheater of these rugged, pine-dotted hills he laid out and planted a series of noble terraces facing the sea.

He was not without help in planning his garden: he had the counsel of the architect Domingo Carles and his wife, the sculptor María Llimona. People also speak of the possible influence of the architect Nicolás María Rubió y Tudurí. First, holes for planting trees had to be dynamited in the rocky ground; then pipes had to be laid to conduct water to the plants; and finally thousands of tons of earth had to be brought in as topsoil. Originally, the Marquess planned a garden that would mature quickly, using species of rapid growth and effect like eucalyptus and mimosa. When a frost killed many of these plants in 1954, he turned to the conifers that form the armature of this garden of luxuriant greenery, among them Italian stone pine, Italian cypress, and Monterey cypress.

That the entire garden is in an impeccable state of preservation is owed to the efforts of Juan Planioll, the chief gardener, who has lived here for fifty years and has made this his life's work. To water the garden, there is a cistern, filled by a well, that holds 21,000 gallons; on some days, it is emptied and filled three times. Once, ten gardeners working every day from eight in the morning until noon raked designs into the sandy paths. Now, it takes one gardener two full days each week to carry out this task, and sixteen days to prune the hedges.

We may say that Santa Clotilde is an Italianate garden "in the Renaissance style," on account of the supremacy accorded to the color green, the extensive use of topiary, and the emphasis on classical sculpture. It would be rash, however, not to consider the dynamism impressed upon it by passion and fantasy, manifest in its slopes and terraces, its flights of stairs, and its maritime aspect. The Marquess was nothing if not attentive to the picturesque values of the landscape, to the point of acquiring the adjacent hills so as to preserve the views from the garden. Nothing that was not "beautiful, sublime, and savage"—to evoke qualities more characteristic of the Romantic era than the Renaissance—would be permitted to intrude upon his work. The many busts and statues of Roman emperors and deities that overlook the sea seem to have come alive.

As a reception room for the garden, there is a large, sandy esplanade, surrounded by tall cypress hedges. This rectilinear space in front of the house, with its four cylindrical cypress trees towering dramatically in the center, has become a symbol of Santa Clotilde. The trees enclose a circular pool, and before them stand marble statues of Justice and Prudence, in Greek antiquity virtues deemed worthy of keeping the gate of the Elysian Fields. The valley that opens below the square toward the sea is no less delightful than the legendary Vale of Tempe. The broad paths and steep flights of steps that connect the different levels of the garden are hedged variously with laurustinus *(Viburnum Tinus),* mock orange *(Pittosporum Tobira),* oleander, and cypress.

The focal point of the slope is the grand staircase that descends to the Plaza de las Sirenas, a space that echoes the esplanade above and is in turn echoed by another, smaller terrace that hangs out over the sea like the prow of a ship. This staircase, stunning in its beauty, is bordered by very tall cypresses and has brick steps, along the risers of which patient fingers have trained ivy. Viewed from the plaza, María Llimona's coquettish green bronze sirens seem to have safely slid their undulating ichthyological bodies down this green cascade to shells of the giant clam *(Tridacna gigas),* which wait at the bottom to transport them seaward. There is no better place to be on a rainy evening, when the wet ivy glitters, the treetops sway, and only the nightingale answers the call to the sirens from the murmuring sea below.

Santa Clotilde

Lloret de Mar
Marchioness of Roviralta de
Santa Clotilde and heirs

Santa Clotilde

Santa Clotilde: The lowest terrace
overlooking the Mediterranean

OPPOSITE
Santa Clotilde: The grand staircase from
the Plaza de las Sirenas

Balearic
Islands

Alfabia

Buñola
José Zaforteza and brothers

THE SIERRA DE Alfabia that rises almost vertically from the sea along the north-west coast of Majorca protects the interior of the island from cold northwest winds. The mountains' southern slopes—covered with Aleppo and Italian stone pines, holly oaks, carob trees, European fan palms, fig trees, Italian cypresses, and mastic trees, to which man has over the centuries added trees bearing dates, Seville oranges, lemons, apples, loquats, almonds, Japanese persimmons, and olives, as well as grapevines—collect rainwater in rivulets that become veritable torrents. This abundance of water accounts for Alfabia, the *alquería,* or farm, which since the days of the Arab occupation of Majorca, has existed beside the road from Palma to Sóller, where it begins its ascent over the range.

Of Arabic origin are the choice of the site; the use of the land for fruit crops; the irrigation canals and reservoirs; the windmills; the use of terraces; and—not least—the name of the property, which for some signifies "jug" and for others "jar," in any case a receptacle for water, necessary for ablution and prayer. Arriving from Arabia and Africa, the followers of Islam invaded Majorca in the eighth century and occupied it for four hundred years, until Jaime I of Aragón set out to reconquer it. To this end he assembled in 1229 such a fleet that the chronicles declared, "The whole sea seemed to be white with sails." In his campaign he was aided by the Moor Ben Afet, the last Arab owner of Alfabia. The victorious king granted the property to his uncle, the Count of Rosellón, who returned it to Ben Afet. It then passed through different branches of Majorca's leading families—Santacilia, Berga, Villalonga—to the Zaforteza family. Over the centuries, it acquired Gothic, Baroque, and Romantic elements.

Access to the estate is provided by a path lined with Spanish sycamores (*Platanus hispanica*) at least ninety years old, which leads to the courtyard of the house, where there is a small fountain. This patio, called a *clastra* in Majorca, is shaded, typ-

Alfabia: The *clastra*

116

ically, by a single tree; a gigantic Spanish sycamore extends its main branches almost horizontally in an offering of protection from the sun. The visitor enters the garden by a straight, gently rising stepped path, also once lined with Spanish sycamores and now bordered by a double row of palm trees and channels of running water, that ends mysteriously at a small patio with a discreet Baroque fountain. The two drowsing nineteenth-century terra-cotta lions on either side of the steps appear to be ineffective guards of a space not worth defending.

On either side of this patio are walled pavilions with identical Baroque windows. One is a *palomar*, or dovecote. The other covers an ancient Arabic *aljibe*, or cistern, with barrel vaulting; arched openings in the near and far walls above the waterline permit a view of the gardens on the other side. The rising path that ends and is blocked on three sides seems theatrically designed to force the visitor to look through the magical eye of the cistern's aperture, and the effect is not unlike the view through a camera lens that gives a small, inverted image: the watery interior receives light only from the rear, through vegetation that nearly blocks the opening. The continuous sound, the luminous darkness, and the reflections constantly stirred by the leaves delight the senses with the simplicity of effect characteristic of the Arabs' architectural genius.

Through a small doorway in the wall beside the fountain, the visitor passes from this patio into the garden, with its vine-covered pergola, of medieval design and Baroque ornamentation. Its steep pebble path descends between low side walls on which rest stone columns, examples of Majorcan Gothic "octagonal" design; these once carried wooden arches that were replaced in the 1930s with metal half-point arches. Intersecting with the pergola are pathways to terraces that were formerly planted with fruit trees but are now planted with ornamentals. At the other end there is a small square patio, which was no doubt covered at some point in the

Alfabia: The patio; looking toward the *palomar*

117

past, with a tablelike stone fountain in the center. The fountain was added in the seventeenth century, as were the twelve pairs of Baroque stone fountainheads placed on the low wall between the columns of the section of the pergola closest to the patio.

Very fine sprays of water emerge with surprising force from barely visible, threadlike piping carved in these fountainheads. These jets, erroneously thought to be of Islamic origin, are actually an invention of the Italian Renaissance. To view the gentle play of water from within the pergola and to see, at the end, the spouting water of the larger fountain—it was said that an orange would balance delicately in the rising stream—spilling down on the table and the ground below is to experience an historic achievement of landscape architecture paralleled only, perhaps, at the Baroque Villa Aldobrandini in Frascati, Italy.

A portion of the gardens adjoining the rear of the house, with paths curving around an artificial lake, was renovated in the nineteenth-century in a style called Romantic or Isabeline, which was inspired by the English landscape garden. The planting makes an exuberant assemblage: windmill palm, thread palm, desert fan palm, wirilda *(Acacia retinodes)*, jacaranda *(J. mimosifolia)*, mimosa *(Albizia Julibrissin)*, timber bamboo *(Phyllostachys bambusoides)*, pampas grass *(Cortaderia Selloana)*, bougainvillea, cape leadwort *(Plumbago auriculata)*, arum lily *(Zantedeschia aethipica)*, Kaffir lily, and water lilies *(Nymphaea alba)* in the pools.

Alfabia: A view toward the lake

OPPOSITE ABOVE
Alfabia: Fountainhead in the pergola

OPPOSITE BELOW
Alfabia: The pergola

S'Avall

Salinas
Carmen Delgado de March

FROM THE EARLIEST times, S'Avall has been favored for human habitation; its earth has revealed remains of ancient necropolises, along with potsherds and slingshot stones. In more recent times, the estate became the property of the Marquess of Palmer and was dedicated to hunting and sheep farming. Apart from a fertile valley, from which the property received the name S'Avall, meaning "valley," the thin soil was too poor for farming. The estate lands equaled 4,444 *cuarteradas,* a magical number if ever there was one. The *cuarterada* is a Majorcan surface measurement equal to about one and three-quarters acres and so the estate covered about 7,780 acres.

Juan March Ordinas bought the property on the southern tip of the island near Cabo Salinas in the early 1930s. Gabriel Alomar, the architect and builder of a palace in Palma de Majorca for the same family, designed a country house here, using stone quarried locally and laid out the first garden along Art Deco lines. Subsequently, Juan March Servera, who inherited the property, enlarged the house and had the garden redesigned. The terrain, except for the area of the valley, was virtually bare rock that had to be covered with topsoil. The whole garden has canals that channel rainwater to underground cisterns, so that not a drop is lost, while drinking water is gathered from the roofs of the buildings, and for several years the estate has had a purification system to desalinate water from the nearby sea. The desire to create and maintain a garden in such adverse conditions is truly admirable.

S'Avall today has both a "Mediterranean" garden—so called because the predominant planting requires the warm temperatures and humidity characteristic of the local climate—and a cactus garden, comprising a total of 2,000 varieties, the vast majority labeled with their botanical names. The Mediterranean garden extends over some seven acres, on a gently sloping terraced terrain, and possesses a typical Majorcan cottage built in miniature and fully furnished for the use of the daughters of the family. Here one finds mastic trees, olive trees, and Aleppo pine, interspersed with more exotic species like jacaranda *(Jacaranda mimosifolia),* Indian laurel *(Ficus retusa),* Moreton Bay fig *(Ficus macrophylla),* white sapote *(Casimiroa edulis),* Brazilian pepper tree *(Schinus terebinthifolius),* and cotton rose *(Hibiscus mutabilis),* with orange flowers. There are also different varieties of crape myrtles, Australian rosemary *(Westringia rosmariniformis),* and above all a cockspur coral tree *(Erythrina crista-galli)* with coral flowers of an unusually deep red that is over forty years old.

S'Avall is famous, and deservedly so, for its cactus collection, which was begun in 1945 in a rather pretentiously arranged rock garden that has an artificial mount with a rising path, a small grotto, and a waterfall. Here, among the cacti, one finds delicate white spider lilies tinged with pink *(Crinum bulbispermum)* and the blue flowers of the heart-shaped pickerelweed *(Pontederia cordata)* from South America. Nearby are sago palms from Madagascar *(Cyca circinalis).* This hill is adorned with circular stones, the old covers of *sixoles,* or underground silos of centuries-old Majorcan tradition, where grain was kept out of the reach of rodents and predators.

In 1958 a new cactus garden of more than three and a half acres was designed by Gabriel Alomar and planted by the horticulturist Juan Pañella Bonastre, today Honorary Director of the Escuela Municipal de Jardinería in Barcelona. The plants covering this great surface are basically those that can thrive in an island climate with high humidity, as those of a more pronounced xerophilic nature cannot survive; because of this, and because the cacti are massed in large groups, the garden does not give the impression of being an arid place; it seems more like a forest than a desert. Among the most spectacular varieties are sea urchin cactus *(Echinopsis validus)* from Bolivia, with one plant over thirty years old; barrel cactus *(Ferocactus peninsulae),* a species that, like a Solomonic column, turns habitually in the same direction as the earth, but at S'Avall possesses the rare quality of turning in the opposite direction; *Cephalocereus polylophus,* with new growth between summer and winter of as many as twenty-eight rings; dragon trees *(Dracaena Draco)* from the Canary Islands; *Pachycereus grandis,* that flowers with spectacular pink trumpets; and creeping devil cactus *(Lemaireocereus Eruca)* from Mexico, which grows by snaking along

the ground and will overcome any obstacle in its horizontal path. There is also a greenhouse for cacti and other crassulaceous plants, where they are studied, reproduced, classified, and acclimated to Majorca, which in general is too humid for these species, under the care of the chief gardener, Antonio Roselló, a true specialist, at the head of a team of ten gardeners.

A cactus garden will always be a green garden; it can have spectacular blooms but they are ephemeral, some lasting only a few hours. It is a garden where silence reigns and there is no shade. The stillness is at times almost threatening. It is with some relief that one reaches the palms that border the cactus garden and the route back to the house, to reexperience the rustling of leaves and the play of light that enliven most gardens as we understand them.

S'Avall: The cactus garden

OPPOSITE ABOVE
S'Avall: The children's cottage

OPPOSITE BELOW
S'Avall: The cactus garden, with the main house in the distance

ONFORTE IS UNUSUAL in that it both moves and pains the visitor at the same time. It evokes the Valencia of the last century and the first twenty years of this one, where wealth was measured in the satisfaction of achievement and life was as coherent as the clear cadences of carriage wheels and horses' hooves on cobblestones.

Monforte was constructed in the mid-nineteenth century as a country house with a garden of some two acres, on the Mediterranean side of the city. Industrialist Juan Bautista Romero (1802–1872), the Marquess of San Juan, chose the flat, square site and enclosed it with high walls, which have since been surpassed in height by skyscrapers. The estate was later inherited by his relative Alvaro Monforte.

The ensemble is customarily described as Neoclassical, accurate as far as it goes, but incomplete as to its garden, where reason and passion vie together in a nineteenth-century expression of the heritage of Rousseau and Goethe. The mansion, surrounded and almost concealed by the garden, expresses within its contained walls a classical feeling of order and measure. In a distant echo of Islamic tradition, the vestibule of the house offers access both to the interior and to two patios that serve as "vestibules" for the garden. The more intimate one is reached by marble stairs that descend to a small square on the opposite side of which is a triumphal gateway crowned by two sea horses and a cornucopia. This small, precise, and cultured space is Neoclassical in feeling, with a central circular pool between borders of boxwood arches. Marble maenads and geese, lambs and swans, imported from Italy, escort the principal figures watching over the garden: Bacchus raising his goblet and squeezing a handful of grapes, and Mercury with a winged helmet, reposing for a minute longer than a century. They represent the spirit of Valencia: enjoyment and industriousness. The more open patio has an outer gate guarded by two marble lions originally created for the Palacio de las Cortes, the Spanish parliament, in Madrid.

MONFORTE

Valencia
Ayuntamiento Municipal de
Valencia

Monforte: The patio dedicated to Bacchus
and Mercury

OPPOSITE
Monforte: Daphnis and Chloe

127

Given their inadequate size for that commission, they were acquired by the Marquess of San Juan to preside over a semicircular space, around the perimeter of which is displayed a collection of marble busts. Dante and Sophocles, Ceres and Flora, overlook a patio perfectly designed for conversation.

Beyond the lion gate, the path leads to a sculpture in white marble of Daphnis and Chloe rising out of a small pool, and this monument is at one of the intersections that form a small grid of six beds of knotted myrtle hedging with a marble allegorical figure in the center of each. The perfumed hedges, composed of the signature species of the garden and treated with topiary art, are of an undeniable beauty. Bordering one side of this Neoclassical knot garden and adjoining one of the perimeter walls is a long, narrow pergola that resembles the Greek stoa. This tunnel of green shade offers a pathway to, and an exquisite perspective of, the larger part of the garden, which seems discordant with the Neoclassical spirit of Monforte, but in reality complements it. For just as the Neoclassical age gave way to the artistic currents of Romanticism, so in Monforte one may leave the formal garden to enter an area composed freely: a garden sinuous, mysterious, and eclectic, where orange trees send their exhalations in homage to divine Hera, whose wedding gift they were.

The artificial mountain symbolizing Mount Nyssa, where Mercury bore Bacchus to save him from evil, is the most important compositional element of the Romantic garden at Monforte. It is an assertion of the superiority of verticality over horizontality, with its play of helicoidal ascent and its changing vistas. Other Romantic elements are the rustic wooden railings, a waterfall, and a hidden grotto. A naturally impossible grove of palm and cypress trees surrounds the mountain, and a curved pool attempts to be a lake, a place of shade and enchantment. The mythological leitmotif at Monforte is water. Its lake, pools, fountains, water nymphs, and dolphins pay homage to Neptune, one of the gods reigning over gardens, for the element vivifying them has its source in him.

Monforte is a garden where symbols are more significant than horticulture, and its language is all but lost to the twentieth century. It was declared a Historic Artistic Garden on May 30, 1943, and became municipal property in 1971.

Monforte: Hibiscus

EL PALMERAL, ONE of the northernmost date-palm groves in the world, was planted by the Phoenicians in what is now the city of Elche, eleven miles south of Alicante. For its survival, we owe a debt of gratitude to Jaime I of Aragón who, when he took the city from the Arabs in 1264, was so captivated with its beauty that he prohibited cutting and burning on the land, the customary medieval punishment to ensure the long-term impoverishment of the vanquished. Neither aridity, nor poor soil, nor salt water, nor the burning sun is the enemy of these palms. Despite urban and industrial development, the grove has multiplied to more than a half-million trees, providing many benefits: the juicy edible fruit; wood; palm leaves for roofs and the manufacture of baskets, rope, and folkloric and religious decorations; and, perhaps the greatest boon of all, shade.

Man showed his gratitude for these simple gifts by cultivating the palm trees in neatly ordered rows forming the blocks that comprise the *huertos*. The planting grid for fruit trees was employed by the Sumerians, Persians, Phoenicians, and Egyptians, and permitted a rational use of soil and light and more efficient irrigation: water reaches the trees in straight canals following a slight gradient (as in the Patios de los Naranjos in Córdoba and Seville). In Spain the cultivation of palm trees is tra-

HUERTO DEL CURA

Elche
José Orts Serrano and brothers

Huerto del Cura: The priest's garden

129

ditionally attributed to the Arabs, who were superb farmers, but it seems to have originated, along with the techniques necessary for their irrigation, in the ancient Near East among the Nabatean people. This knowledge was zealously applied by the Arabs, who extended the practice throughout their dominions.

Since the Middle Ages, the central areas of the Palmeral have been devoted to other crops that yielded a greater return. These spaces were enclosed with simple palm fences and became redoubts of shade and humidity, which motivated the owners or caretakers to build houses and create gardens. Paradoxically, horticulture takes us away from nature and the natural disposition of its basic elements: living organisms, earth and water, light and air. This process, almost as old as history itself, can be seen in the evolution of Elche from date-palm groves to *huertos,* and then, in some cases, to gardens.

Huerto del Cura: Fountain with a reproduction of the Dama de Elche, an ancient Iberian sculpture found in Elche

In 1843, two events took place in a *huerto* that belonged to the Castaño family, who grew pomegranates and artichokes among the palms: a son was born (the second in the family) and a singular palm tree that was to influence the course of his life germinated amidst all the others. The boy, José Castaño, grew up to be a priest, or *cura,* and eventually inherited the *huerto* where he was raised; the tree, after about thirty years, began to produce shoots around its trunk at about six feet above ground level. This phenomenon was observed with curiosity, for palms develop shoots that grow around the base, not above. Palm trees are dioecious, which means that the female plants, which bear the fruit, have to be fertilized with the pollen of the male plants; the pollen is carried by wind, birds, and insects. The unusual palm tree with seven branches in the Huerto del Cura was the only male plant in the *huerto* to have produced its own offspring. It has been the focus of international attention ever since this rare growth pattern was first observed in 1873.

In 1894, the Empress Elizabeth of Austria accompanied by her first cousin Archduke Louis Salvador visited the garden incognito. She saw for herself the unusual palm and suggested to Castaño that he give the tree a specific name, which he did, calling it the Palmera Imperial to commemorate the visit by the sovereign. Since then, it has become a singular custom in Elche to give female palm trees names of famous personalities: Flammarion, Pérez Galdós, Debussy, La Mistinguette, Sert, Unamuno, Cortázar, and Rubinstein are notable examples. By 1900, the Huerto del Cura was well enough known that a group of scientists who were in Elche to view a total solar eclipse came to visit and admire it. In 1918 Castaño died and the *huerto* was acquired the next year by his friend Juan Orts Miralles, to whose family the property has since belonged. The new owner scheduled tours of what he called the Huerto Imperial, though in popular speech it continued to be called the Huerto del Cura. A series of photographic postcards was printed, and the fame of the *huerto* spread beyond the borders of Spain.

The Huerto del Cura passed into the hands of Juan Orts Roman in 1940. He fixed up the house, constructing a porch supported by palm trunks and decorated with large pots of calla lilies, installed an *alberca* for irrigation, and added flowering plants to the garden. Until the 1950s, the garden's paths were edged with lattices of thin reeds; it is known that some unusual eighteenth-century gardens had this feature, reflecting the vogue for Chinoiserie, and its reintroduction would be interesting.

In 1958 the *huerto* was inherited by the children of Juan Orts and Dolores Serrano. One of them, José Orts Serrano, has devoted his life to horticulture. He founded a nursery and gardening center, opened a campsite, and built a luxury hotel, all in the date-palm grove of Elche, but his chief interest has always been the Huerto del Cura. Its character, since the mid-1960s, has become increasingly exotic, and the newly planted *huerto* is now famous for its collection of cacti. The Palmera Imperial has survived for half its normal life span of 300 years; supporting its seven supplementary trunks is an indispensable metal brace to sustain its ten-ton weight. El Palmeral was declared a National Monument and the Huerto del Cura a National Historic Garden on July 15, 1948.

Huerto del Cura: The Palmera Imperial

Huerto del Cura: The cactus garden, with
another rare palm specimen

Andalucía

La Alhambra

Granada
Patronato de la Alhambra y
Generalife

La Alhambra: The Torre de Comares, with
the Sierra Nevada in the background

OPPOSITE ABOVE
La Alhambra: The Patio de los Arrayanes;
looking toward the Torre de Comares

OPPOSITE BELOW
La Alhambra: The Patio de los Arrayanes

PTOLEMY, WHOSE NAME was synonymous with geographical knowledge for fifteen hundred years, was himself stirred by Granada's dramatic setting, in the foothills of the Sierra Nevadas, the highest mountains in the Iberian peninsula, from whose snowy peaks life-giving water descends in three rivers, Genil, Darro, and Beiro, to the *vega*, the limitless fertile plain with its luxuriant groves. The city is set on seven hills, one of which, the Assabika hill, the "hill of red earth," is the Alhambra's.

La Alhambra, which means "the red one," was virtually a city itself, a lofty fortress defended by massive ramparts and prismatic towers; in its precincts, where the sultans of Spain's Nazrid dynasty (1238–1492) built their palaces, the oldest surviving Islamic gardens in the world can be enjoyed today. Seven centuries ago, even the sides of the hill were covered with groves and gardens and there were numerous canals to distribute the racing waters brought in by aqueducts from the mountains that were always in view.

Within the palace complex there exist at least two principal courtyard gardens, dating from the fourteenth century, that are worth lingering over, for their forms profoundly influenced many subsequent Spanish gardens. The older, and perhaps the more beautiful, of the two, the Patio de los Arrayanes, or Patio de la Alberca, was created by Yusuf I (1333–54) and was the court of ablutions before his throne room in the Torre de Comares.

The spare elegance of the Patio de los Arrayanes, and particularly the rigor of its planting, both startle the visitor and account for its singular transcendental ambience. The patio measures 120 by 75 feet, and its central feature is an oblong *alberca*

134

La Alhambra: The Patio de los Leones

that is almost precisely one-third as wide as the patio and runs almost its entire length. The long sides of the *alberca* are bordered by straight hedges of fragrant myrtle, *arrayán* in Spanish. The general lines of composition are insistently longitudinal and parallel. Between the hedging and the *alberca,* the myrtle and the water, are dramatic corridors made of slabs of white marble. The long, smooth enclosing walls, with their tiny *ajimeces,* or couple-arched windows, contained public rooms for the courtiers. These walls—today bare—are said to have been painted with scenes of dancers amidst flowers and trees, similar to murals that survive in other Arabic palaces, and a Venetian ambassador found citrus trees in the patio in 1526. Each end of the court is screened by a graceful alabaster colonnade supporting an arcade of intricately carved stucco. At either end of the pool is a circular marble basin flush with the ground; in the Arabic fashion, water burbles quietly from the center of each without raising a jet into the air. These evoke a distant naturalism; a hint of the lotuses of Egypt. The marble floor slopes gently toward the water, subtly recalling the Roman *impluvium,* and, indeed, in its use of space, the patio echoes the classical peristyle.

The ideas suggested by this garden are as complex as the space itself is simple. The nearly motionless *alberca* reflects the rugged mass of the battlemented tower and offers a yielding horizontal counterpoise to its uncompromising vertical thrust, symbolic of the earthly power of the sultan. In theological terms, it provides yet another pathway to the eye for the stellar light of the heavenly paradise revealed by the Koran. Furthermore, for all their abstract quality, Islamic gardens must be considered as spaces intended primarily to appeal to the senses of the devout visitor, conducing to inwardness and union with God (in Islam, all arts lead to prayer, and the garden was the paramount influence in Muslim art). In the Patio de los Arrayanes, the two sunken fountains at the ends of the pool catch the

attention of both the eye and the ear: the water fills each stone basin in a fine, spreading sheet and then escapes into the *alberca* at greater speed down a narrow conduit, where it undulates in constantly changing, endlessly repeated, mesmerizing lines.

La Alhambra: The Patio de los Leones

The tangible image of temporal majesty that Yusuf I placed before every ambassador ushered into his presence by way of the Patio de los Arrayanes was not the impression his son Muhammad V (1354–59 and 1362–91) wished his cultured court to impart. This monarch surrounded himself with artists and writers, even appointing them to high administrative positions. Beginning in 1377, Muhammad V built his own palace beside that of his predecessor, without the present-day connecting passage between them. The palace is organized around an arcaded garden area, measuring ninety-two feet by fifty-two feet, named the Patio de los Leones, or Patio of the Lions, for the twelve archaic looking beasts that seem to bear the central fountain basin on their backs. One hundred twenty-four slender alabaster columns support the arcades, and two airy pavilions, roofed with wood, project into the enclosure.

The Persian pleasure garden, whose form was adopted for the Patio de los Leones, was an enclosed space intersected by four watercourses, symbolizing the holy rivers Tigris, Euphrates, Gihon, and Fison. The quadrants demarcated by these streams were associated with the four basic elements: air, water, earth, and fire. The nomadic Arabs, always in search of oases, found in the gardens of sixth-century Persia, which they conquered, the paradise promised by Allah to all believers, a place of flowing waters, boundless fruit, and above all shade. (Their word for a "garden," signifying an enclosed space, is "paradise.") Despite the Koranic warning "Woe be to him who enjoys paradise in this life," the Arabs went on to build paradise gardens from the Ganges River in India to the Ebro in Spain. Thus, a garden plan that had been brought to perfection under Persia's Sassanid dynasty was perpetuated and refined by the followers of Islam in fourteenth-century Spain.

If the Patio de los Arrayanes is centripetal in its organization of space, relying on the reflecting *alberca* to erase the sensation of far and near, the Patio de los Leones exhibits a centrifugal plan. As in the Persian paradise garden, streams of water emanate in four directions from the central fountain. Four little canals accentuating the main axes carry the overflow to each side of the patio: to the Sala de las Dos Hermanas and the Sala de los Abencerrajes, to the north and south respectively; and as far as the forecourts of the Sala de los Mocárabes and the Sala de los Reyes, to the west and east. Among the Arabs, the lion, symbolic of royalty, was the preferred animal for zoomorphic fountains. In all known cases, water dribbles from the jaws of these beasts like "the spittle of their mouths." When water advances from the lion fountain, it meets and mingles with water running in the opposite direction from the small fountains in the buildings on each side. The constant splashing of the central fountain's jet and the murmur of the water coursing through the channels are remarkably pleasing to the senses.

It is thought that the ground in the four quadrants of the Patio de los Leones was originally about thirty inches below the level of the marble pathways, and that in these sunken spaces were beds of flowering plants, resembling Persian carpets (a visitor in 1602 found six orange trees in each one, but this was already a departure from the original planting). Nothing, however, was allowed to break the plane of the pathways, so that the lions might maintain supremacy in their kingdom. In the stucco of the Sala de las Dos Hermanas are inscribed the words, "I am the garden that adorns beauty. You will know of me if you contemplate my beauty . . . we never bespied so flowering a garden of sweeter harvest or more fragrance." If, as the poet Antonio Machado declared, the Alhambra represents hidden water that weeps, the Patio de los Leones, presently filled with gravel, thirsts for its lost plants!

The real secret of the beauty of the Patio de los Leones is the rapidly changing light, which imparts to everything a feeling of weightlessness, transforming stone and water into a landscape for the soul. The profusion of columns and the play of light and shadow in the arcades bring to mind a *palmeral,* or date-palm grove; the presence of water in the center evokes an oasis; the two pavilions advance into the patio like nomadic tents. Thus we are transported, as if by a magic carpet of the collective unconscious, from a desert oasis to a Nazrid palace.

To the east of the Palacio de los Leones was a third palace called the Partal, of which there survives the high portico that was added to the defensive ramparts of the Assabika by Muhammad III (1302–09) and an adjoining *alberca,* watered by jets in the jaws of two large, seated stone lions, that is the largest reservoir of the Islamic era in the Alhambra.

Extensive terraced gardens surround the royal palaces and their many outbuildings, exemplary of the architecture of medieval Islamic Spain. The gardens, which cover much of the high ground to the south and east of the Palacio del Partal, are innovative twentieth-century creations, dating from 1924. They are the work of Modesto Cendoya and Leopoldo Torres Balbás, the architects who restored the Alhambra. After studying the whole area, they decided to preserve without restoring the ruined foundations of a number of other palatial buildings that once occupied the site. In their essence, the pools and the plantings amidst these low, broken walls recall the Hispano-Islamic garden. Time, the coauthor of gardens, has rendered a favorable verdict. Cypresses and poplars emerge haughtily between hedges of cypress, myrtle, and boxwood. There is a profusion of color and fragrance. And while the planting is not absolutely authentic, at least it gives an Islamic impression, with tulips, anemones, buttercups, common melilot, narcissus, lilies of the valley, violets, carnations, marshmallow, hyacinths, wallflowers, primroses, saffron, lilacs, irises, delphiniums, and tuberoses. Absent are the various species of fruit trees that were indispensable to the Arabs. In 1870, the Alhambra was declared a Historic Artistic Monument.

La Alhambra: The Jardines de Partal

El Generalife

Granada
Patronato de la Alhambra y
Generalife

LOCATED ON THE shoulder of the hill called Cerro del Sol, the Hill of the Sun, which is higher than the Assabika and separated from it by a gorge, are the gardens of the Generalife. The fact that they are the oldest in Granada is known to few who follow the conventional tour that begins with the later Islamic gardens in the palace complex of La Alhambra. The Generalife, finished in 1319 by the Sultan Isma'il I (1314–25), is not a palatial residence; it was built as a country house, with its own pleasure gardens, at the heart of an *almunia*, an estate on which it depended for the fruit, vegetables, and simples that were grown there.

According to scholars, "El Generalife" signifies variously "the garden of al-Arife" or "unequaled garden." *Jinnah-al-arif* are words that may mean either a garden or an architect of great stature. In this reading, both the garden and its designer are equally "high profile," and we may see here a model attempt to emulate the garden promised by Allah as a prize for the just.

The situation of the Generalife on lands belonging to the sultan outside the fortified hilltop enclosure of the Alhambra suggests that originally it may not have been intended to be a permanent installation but was gradually planted as more land was required for food production. The natural slope of the hill was terraced in order to achieve a useful horizontality and there exist vestiges of the ramparts enclosing the site that give an idea of its original perimeter. Its *acequias,* or irrigation canals, both open channels and underground conduits, conveyed four times the volume of those of the Alhambra, a clear indication that the water was needed to irrigate food crops. The Acequia del Tercio was the highest; the Acequia del Rey was the lowest; and, in the middle, was the Acequia del Generalife, each one following the level curves of the terraces facing the Alhambra. The original *huertas*, or orchards, called La Mercería, La Colorada, La Grande, and Fuentepeña, were planted on terraces separated by considerable drops in height of up to twenty-three feet.

It was in the *huertas* of the Generalife that the Arabs of al-Andalus put to good use the profound horticultural knowledge that they disseminated throughout medieval Europe, a knowledge based both on practice and on their translations of the Greek, Nabatean, Persian, Egyptian, Byzantine, and Roman texts that formed the basis of their agricultural treatises. One of these works, written in the twelfth century, named twenty varieties of vegetables, twenty-five varieties of fruit, and thirty varieties of herbs and spices. Time has almost totally erased the productive aspect of the *huertas* in the Generalife. Just as the Patio de los Leones in the Alhambra demands that its plantings be restored, so the Generalife begs to have back its orchards and vegetable gardens. Robbed of their context, the patios of the Generalife may be admired but cannot be fully appreciated.

Access to the Generalife was originally gained by one of two approaches. The direct one, an uphill path that still exists but is rarely used, went from the Alhambra, through the gate at the foot of the Torre de los Picos, crossed the Camino de los Muertos in the ravine between the two hills, now the Cuesta de los Chinos, and entered the Generalife between high walls as a narrow, moatlike cobble lane. This bowered path provided a rapid, secret entrance leading to the small summer villa for the sultans that has partly disappeared. The other approach, in the area called Fuentepeña, is today the main entrance and ushers the visitor through the twentieth-century additions to the garden, whose horticultural character distantly echoes their original function.

In what remains of the royal villa the visitor encounters an entrance patio with remnants of vine arbors for shade and a narrow staircase by which one reaches the *riat,* or enclosed garden, called the Patio de la Acequia. The garden's proportions are imposed by the natural incline of the ground; it is, in essence, a planted terrace. The long, narrow enclosure with buildings on three sides and an arcaded walk on the fourth is a cruciform garden of Persian inspiration, centered on a 162-foot-long, 4-foot-wide *acequia,* a stone-edged canal with flowing water. There is a much shorter arm that crosses it, forming quadrants of myrtle and orange trees. Built into the arcaded walk on the long western side of the patio was a central pavilion,

OPPOSITE ABOVE
El Generalife: View of the Albaicín from the northern pavilion

OPPOSITE BELOW
El Generalife: The Patio de la Acequia from the northern pavilion

140

covered with roses, in which the sultan could contemplate the garden. Gabriel Alonso de Herrera, who published the *Libro de agricultura general* in 1513, had been a twenty-two-year-old student in Granada in 1492, when the city fell to the Christian forces, and he never forgot "the capricious forms in which the Granadan Moors clipped the myrtles in the royal palace and the house of the Generalife." Significant alterations were made to this garden and the surrounding buildings in the Renaissance and the Romantic period. With some loss of intimacy, the arcaded walk was opened up with bays and the pavilion at the center converted to a belvedere overlooking the Alhambra, and galleries were superimposed on the royal pavilion to the north. The planting has been changed several times; today the beds are less cluttered than they were as recently as the first quarter of this century. But the jets that were added to the canal in the last century continue to disturb the primal peace of the Patio de la Acequia.

The anachronistic sounds of splashing water leads the visitor on to another enclosed garden called the Patio de los Cipreses or the Patio de la Sultana. In this interesting patio, renovated in the sixteenth century and again in the nineteenth, when a profusion of waterspouts of Romantic inspiration was added, one finds square, moated plots of oleander. Ascending a staircase enclosed by walls, one reaches a higher terrace that forms the beginning of the Romantic garden, strongly Italian in feeling: not in vain was the title to this estate transferred from the Venegas family to the Grimaldis, from whom it was recovered by the Spanish government in 1921, thanks to the intercession of King Alfonso XIII.

Surprisingly, in this area survives an original Nazrid element, hardly altered

El Generalife: The Paseo de los Cipresses

since it was constructed by the Moors: the Escalera de Agua, or water staircase, of modest dimensions and built with simple materials: lime, stone, bricks, and roof tiles. It is narrow, barely wide enough for two persons, rising in three sections with, at each level, open, circular areas enclosed by low sidewalls where one can stop one's climb to contemplate the falling water. These walls have on their tops glass tiles of green and turquoise that form channels, down which water races tumultuously, splashing noisily in the angles formed by the different levels of the stairs, to an irrigation canal below. The Escalera del Agua once had a central channel that, in an unfortunate "improvement" for the sake of the visitor, was removed.

Since these stairs offer a passage to a higher garden, the sound of falling water here defines an interval; it eliminates prior sounds and prepares the visitor for the silence to be regained at the top. The change of light effected by the passage is also significant: one passes through a vault of laurel, a tunnel of green shade more dazzling than the sky itself. This rapid, absolute change induces in the visitor feelings of inexpressible wonder and delight.

By far the largest part of the gardens of the Generalife were designed in the 1950s by Prieto Moreno, the architect-curator of the Alhambra. Several terraces of the gardens were consolidated for the installation of an open-air theater. Elsewhere, the greater area was divided into Italianate compartments, or cabinets, of greenery; spaces of pseudo-Islamic inspiration, with cypress hedging and neo-Romantic pools; a veritable orgy of flowers and fragrances. The nineteenth century bequeathed two elements forming this space with great skill: a tunnel of oleander and the Paseo de los Cipresses, an avenue of cypresses inaugurated in 1862 on the occasion of a state visit by Queen Isabella II. Already more than a century old, this majestic passage grows more beautiful every year.

OPPOSITE ABOVE
El Generalife: The Patio de la Acequia

OPPOSITE BELOW
El Generalife: The Patio de los Cipreses

El Albaicín and the Carmen de los Cipreses

Granada
Joaquín López

THE HILL BORDERING the north bank of the Río Darro, across from the Alhambra and the Generalife, is called the Albaicín. The Arabic word *Albayzin* derives from *Rabad al-Bayyazin*, signifying "quarter on the hill." Numerous houses, a mosque, and an *alcazaba,* or fort, were built on the Albaicín in the eleventh century. As the latter was constructed before the Alhambra, it was known as the Alcazaba Qadima or old fort. Some vestiges of the mosque, considered the most beautiful in Granada, are found in the sixteenth-century church of El Salvador that was built on its site, in particular the garden planted with lemon trees. This, like the bell tower of San Juan de los Reyes, which incorporates a thirteenth-century minaret, is an example of the integration of Islamic with Castilian culture; of what in Spanish culture appears shared yet in reality is denied. This sense of cultural fusion constitutes the essence of the Albaicín.

The Albaicín today retains its medieval atmosphere, with lanes so narrow that the housetops join above them while below two donkeys could not pass. Seen from the Alhambra and the Generalife, it presents a unique view of houses interwoven with gardens, the pink surfaces of roofs and the prismatic whites of façades, punctuated by the evergreen forms of Italian cypress. The small houses, or *carmens,* which were once inhabited by the Arabs, are surrounded by patios, gardens, and *huertos* and

enclosed by high walls bordered by narrow, tortuous, and ever-so-steep lanes that are more often merely stairs. This miniaturization of spaces and structures lends liveliness to the urban landscape.

The *carmen* is peculiar to Granada, like the *can* in Catalonia, the *son* in Majorca, the *cigarral* in Toledo, the *pazo* in Galicia, the *masía* in Valencia, and the *hocino* in Cuenca; all signify some form of cultivated land, and each has its distinguishing characteristics. A *carmen* (the word derives from the sixteenth-century Castilian form of the Arabic word *karm*, meaning grapevine or vineyard) is a house, well protected and relatively small, with a garden and *huerto* attached. We have often, in this book, cause to lament the disappearance of traditional *huertos*, with their blending of fruit trees, vegetables, simples, and ornamentals, even in "restored" gardens. Happily, at the Carmen de los Cipreses, the *huerto* remains.

Carmens can be found scattered throughout the *vega* and in the hills surrounding the city of Granada. The terraced hillside *carmens* take the form of a series of small, superimposed planes. After the Reconquest, this Hispano-Islamic tradition survived the general rural decline of the seventeenth and eighteenth centuries. In the nineteenth century, the orientalist fervor of Romanticism gave new life to the *carmen*, which came to be celebrated as the typical Granadan private home.

Carmen de los Cipreses: The *alberca*

BELOW
Carmen de los Cipreses: The *mirador*

BELOW RIGHT
Carmen de los Cipreses: The pergola

The Albaicín is covered with these small estates, protected by high walls of stucco covered with hanging flowers, behind which trees laden with fruit soar toward the heavens. Each is a tiny world with its own marvels and peculiarities. And each is truly privileged, if for no other reason than that it looks out upon the Alhambra.

The Carmen de los Cipreses is a perfect example. The house is small, centered on a patio with a typically Granadan stone floor, paved in black and white. The upper floors open out into galleries that overlook this patio, whose ivy-covered walls create a well of greenery, coolness, and shade. From the house, the land descends in terraces. A grove of Italian cypresses—a favorite species in the Persian gardens so admired by the Arabs—screens the largest and uppermost level, where the *alberca* that waters the property is located. One finds here fruit-bearing trees, such as the date palm, Japanese persimmon, orange, and loquat, and an *emparrado*, or vine arbor, along with southern magnolias. Shading the terrace, and offering a spectacular view of the Alhambra, is a pergola covered with Banksia roses. Here, at the end of the last century, the *carmen*'s previous owner, Nicolás María López, hosted an informal literary circle that included his friend the famous writer Angel Ganivet (1865–1898).

Accompanied by the fragrance of Spanish jasmine *(Jasminum grandiflorum)* and roses, one descends from level to level, by short, narrow flights of stairs. Toward the bottom of the garden, fruit trees predominate—pomegranate, quince, common fig, orange, and pear—as well as laurel and vegetables. There are seven levels, as in the garden of the poet Pedro Soto de Rojas (c. 1584–c. 1658), who was born on the Albaicín in the Carmen de los Mascarones. Rojas combined in his garden design Moorish tradition, Renaissance learning, and Baroque expressive values. There were seven levels, which he called *"moradas"* ("dwelling places"), that together would constitute a book in which one could read the message that every garden holds: the transformation of the Koranic "paradise closed to many" into a "paradise open to all."

Carmen de los Cipreses: The view of the Alhambra from the pergola

ON THE SOUTHERN side of Granada's Assabika hill, there are several villas with panoramic views of the *vega* and the Sierra Nevada. On the steepest part of the slope, known as the Monte Mauror, the painter José Rodríguez Acosta built, in 1914–20, an astonishing studio/villa, a Cubistic house of cards, which became a museum after his death in 1941. The Carmen de la Fundación Rodríguez Acosta is a creation in rhythm with the twentieth century that also evokes, through its notable collection of classical sculpture, the remote civilization of imperial Rome.

Great stepped retaining walls follow the precipitous incline of the hill, and the garden courts are enclosed by arcaded walls. Villa and garden are here almost equally architectural in feeling, to the extent that the biological aspect of the plants is almost denied and the only clear difference between man-made walls and natural walls is one of color: white speaks for the house, limpid and inanimate; green for the garden, mysterious, profound, and organic.

In this rigorous, Hadrianesque garden Italian cypress and boxwood reign triumphant, and the visitor can easily imagine ancient philosophers disputing within these fragrant rooms. No other tree than the cypress could attain the necessary height without obscuring the view, nor could another lend itself to the pre-established shapes of topiary art, the legacy of Rome, that form the basis of this Spanish garden. Green pavilions of structured space echo the geometry of the villa, from the base of which they advance down the hillside in terraces, almost doubling the terrain in a spectacular feat of spatial design. These open out to a vast landscape but preserve for the solitary visitor a Moorish sense of intimacy.

Rodríguez Acosta made, in his villa and garden, an ideal spot for each of the art objects that he collected: the numerous sixteenth- and seventeenth-century columns, and others of Nazrid origin; Roman and Baroque sculptures, both originals and copies; medieval and Renaissance architectural ornaments. It is not strange that this villa ended up as a museum for it was born as one, and its collections were incorporated into its very construction. Of floral displays, on the other hand, there are few: ivy geranium *(Pelargonium peltatum)* or *gitanilla* spills over an antique amphora set in a corner, looking rather like a bullfighter's abandoned cape; while bright red and faded yellow roses provide their accents of color and fragrance to the pergola-covered balcony, presided over by Diana, who has her back turned to the city of Granada laid out below, while in another, enclosed area of the garden, a poolside Venus appears secure in the knowledge that no mortal will ever be able to contemplate her nakedness.

CARMEN DE LA FUNDACIÓN RODRÍGUEZ ACOSTA

Granada
Junta de Andalucía

Carmen de la Fundación Rodríguez Acosta

Carmen de la Fundación Rodríguez
Acosta: Venus

Carmen de la Fundación Rodríguez
Acosta: Diana

JARDINES DE NARVÁEZ

Loja
Julia Díaz Berbel de Díaz
Jiménez

NARVÁEZ OWES ITS long-standing fame to its nineteenth-century owner, General Ramón María de Narváez, Duke of Valencia (1800–1868), who was born in Loja and is buried in the chapel on the estate. It is an excellent example of an Andalusian *cortijo*: there are a house for the owners when they are in residence and lands devoted mainly to the cultivation of olive trees, with a *huerta* irrigated by canals in the traditional Islamic fashion. The sturdy, two-story house has whitewashed walls and a roof of Arabic tile, while the interior is designed with Isabeline delicacy. The remains of an old mill have been found on the property.

It is, however, chiefly the Romantic garden, with its distinctly Spanish touches, created during General Narváez's life that draws the visitor here. It extends behind the house, parallel to the *huerta* and separated from it by an older garden called the Jardín Antiguo. This pleasure garden is laid out with numerous fountains and two paths that are virtually tunnels of laurel, but is most remarkable for its freeform island beds enclosed by sinuous hedges of neatly trimmed boxwood.

Hedges of traditional species cut in dynamic and even capricious forms are characteristic of the Romantic gardens that proliferated in Spain during the nineteenth century and the first years of the twentieth. The little, hedged-in island beds of Narváez, with their accumulation of eclectic plants, all arranged to fit a small, level site, are a Spanish variation on the larger island beds inset in rolling lawns that had their origin in eighteenth-century England, where the landscape garden was born. It is thought that this garden may have been designed by gardeners employed by the Crown, which is certainly possible, given the Duke of Valencia's closeness to the royal family and the resemblance of his garden to others by François Vié, a French gardener who worked on royal and noble gardens, among them the Palacio de Oca.

Jardines de Narváez

152

ACURIOUS RULE of thumb in Córdoba is that the size of the patio—that virtual-ly ubiquitous element of domestic architecture imported to Spain by the Romans, who in turn, got it from the Greeks—is almost always in inverse relation to the number of persons living in a building. This is not to say that the city is without those substantial patios resembling the Roman peristyle, consisting of a courtyard surrounded by a colonnade or arcade, so characteristic of Seville; it is just that its spirit dwells in those patios content to evoke the memory of the atrium, a modest open area that mediates between the interior rooms and the street. The nar-row lanes and small houses of Córdoba tend naturally to yield tiny patios that func-tion both as intimate stages for the private dramas of daily life and as public spaces where the occupants of the house encounter visitors from the world outside its walls. A subtle social code that can be read in a closed outer gate, a door left ajar, or sim-ply a drawn curtain manages to ease any tensions that may arise out of these two conflicting uses. We can find in the highly sophisticated, contemporary garden designs of the Brazilian Roberto Burle Marx (b. 1909) an echo of these tiny Cordoban patios with their distinctive "plantings." The typical patio, by the way, is to be found in the working-class section of the *Juderia,* Córdoba's ancient Jewish quarter.

The small Cordoban patio is indeed like a stage, and as on a stage, every ele-ment takes on almost exaggerated importance to those who exist in it: the doors, the stairs (if there are more than one, and in that case upper galleries as well), interior windows that open onto it, a well or a fountain, a washbasin. The leading roles go to the women, for it is here that they perform many of their daily domestic chores. To keep such small spaces tidy requires an extreme economy of means and func-tions. The Cordobans have compensated themselves for this necessary emphasis on simplicity and austerity by decorating their patios with flowers.

The reduced space is cared for to the point of pampering: constantly swept; washed down and whitewashed with almost ritualistic fervor as a defensive measure against the heat of the sun (this domestic task is carried out so often that fine layers of lime and salt build up, softening the contours of every corner). Given the intense foot traffic that such a space must bear, the cobblestone floors are rarely available for garden beds. Flowerpots are arranged on any horizontal surface where they will not get in the way of daily chores, and when this space is exhausted, they are hung on the walls themselves, transforming them into vertical gardens of mainly red and pink flowers whose intense hues harmonize with their green leaves and stand out strikingly against the white background. In the humblest of patios, where ceramic pots are not to be had, tin cans are employed, lending a beautiful use to an other-wise useless object.

The laborious daily watering required by these gardens in hot weather is, of course, also woman's work, as is everything relating to love and fantasy. The most characteristic flower used for this idiosyncratically Spanish custom comes from South Africa: the ivy geranium *(Pelargonium peltatum)*. Also much in evidence are *P. zonale* and *P. x domesticum,* prized for the black spots on its petals. On the ground, in flowerpots, we find carnations *(Dianthus Caryophyllus),* impatiens *(I. Wallerana),* yellow sage *(Lantana Camara),* calla lilies, and umbrella plants *(Cyperus alternifolius).* If there is a little pool, basil and spearmint for soups and salads are likely to be perched on its edge. And in a corner, climbing on any available support, is poet's jas-mine *(Jasminum officinale)* or night jasmine *(Cestrum nocturnum)* for fragrance.

Each year, in mid-May, everyone in Córdoba takes great pleasure in partici-pating in the festival known as the Cruz de Mayo, in which prizes are awarded to the best patios.

Patios, Córdoba

PATIO DE LOS NARANJOS

Seville
Archbishopric of Seville

CONSTRUCTION OF THE mosque of Seville began in 1172, under the rule of the Caliph Abu Ya'cub Yusuf (1139–1184), who from his childhood kept the memory of the example of the Great Mosque of Córdoba. After the conquest of Seville by King Ferdinand III of Castile and León (1217–52) in 1248, it was used for Christian worship, and it was almost totally obliterated by the construction of a cathedral in the fifteenth century. Only the minaret, now the cathedral's tower, and the Patio de los Naranjos, which was the *sahn,* or courtyard, of the mosque, remain.

The three-hundred-foot-high minaret, from which the faithful were summoned to prayer, was topped with a terrace facing the four cardinal directions and was decorated with four golden spheres—diminishing in size—that shone resplendently. In their place we now find the famous figured weather vane, or *giraldillo,* of 1568 after which the landmark tower is named: La Giralda.

The patio itself is not what it was in Islamic times, having been marginalized by the great Gothic cathedral without providing access to it. Enclosed by high walls, the space induced in worshipers a proper state of mind during the time that it took to traverse it to the mosque. Sharp-pointed horseshoe arches screened a portico that followed the perimeter of the patio on three sides; on the fourth similar arches opened into the mosque, from where the trees of the *sahn* would have been visible. Each outer wall had an entrance to the patio, of which only the Puerta del Perdón, to the north, survives, in much-altered condition. The delicately paved brick patio, centered on a fountain-basin, reflects the austerity of the Almohads, Berbers from North Africa who by the mid-twelfth century, when, coincidentally, Saint Bernard had imposed a similarly severe spirit in Cistercian architecture, had succeeded in establishing Seville as a capital of Arab culture rivaling Córdoba.

The patio is planted with straight rows of orange trees that continued the lines established by the interior columns, as in Córdoba; the floor was sunk below ground level, with a rectilinear pattern of *acequias* to water each tree. The space is a symbolic expression of the Koran's promise of fruit, flowers, shade, and water as a reward for the faithful and was once planted mainly with olive trees, as well as Italian cypresses and date palms, all of which in time were replaced with orange trees.

Viewed from the Giralda, the rounded tops of the orange trees in the former *sahn* of the mosque of Seville cast circles of dense shade, today welcoming no one: they stand silently, yearning for the devout of yesteryear. From the Giralda, one can also see the Reales Alcazares, which once served as a fortified residence of the Moorish kings for whom it was built. Its famous Moorish gardens, much altered since they were first laid out a hundred years after the Reconquest of the Almohad capital in 1248, were the work of Arab craftsmen.

A view of the Reales Alcazares from the Giralda of Seville cathedral

OPPOSITE
Patio de los Naranjos

On September 27, 1483, Pedro Enríquez, Governor of Andalucía, and his wife, Catalina de Ribera, acquired property in Seville possessing a *huerta*, baker's mill, and running water from the Roman aqueduct known as the Caños de Carmona, the latter a sign of both the high esteem in which the owners were held and the value of the *huerta*: the flowing water was the property of the king and its possession a privilege. Not finding the land sufficient for their needs, in 1484 the powerful Riberas purchased adjacent land, with a palace and gardens, from the Pinedas family, in need of money to ransom a son held hostage by the Moors in Granada. These properties came to be divided into two estates, one of which became the Casa de Pilatos.

Fadrique Enríquez de Ribera, the first Marquess of Tarifa, was primarily responsible for the grandeur of the Casa de Pilatos and the quality of its decoration, much of which he commissioned on a long journey through Renaissance Italy. Thus, it was Antonio María Aprile of Genoa who created, in 1529, numerous columns, two fountains, a triumphal portal, and the family sepulchers. Various Roman and Greek sculptures were sent from Italy later in the sixteenth century, when Per Afan Enríquez de Ribera was Viceroy of Naples, at which time the architect Benvenuto Tortello laid out a garden, now called the Jardín Grande, on the site of the former *huerta* and added galleries and loggias. The house came by its unusual name after a pilgrimage by the first Marquess to Jerusalem in 1519 gave rise to the popular belief that the plan of Pontius Pilate's Pretorium in Jerusalem served as a model for the new palace, formerly called the Palacio de San Andrés, after the patron saint of the family. The palace itself is a masterpiece of sixteenth-century Hispanic architecture in which Gothic, Mudéjar, and Renaissance elements linking Christian, Islamic, and humanist influences are perfectly integrated. When Fernando Enríquez de Ribera, third Duke of Alcalá de los Gazules and a son of the Viceroy, decided to reside permanently in the palace, he enlarged it to install his small court of thirty-three persons, including doctors, musicians, astrologers, and librarians to tend his fine collection of classical manuscripts. Under him the palace became a center of Spanish culture, where the leading painters and writers, among them Cervantes (1547–1616), always found a welcome.

The Casa de Pilatos passed to the Medinaceli family in 1625 with the marriage of the last female heir, Ana Luisa Enríquez de Ribera, to Juan Luis de La Cerda, seventh Duke of Medinaceli. The family lived in an immense palace in Madrid, which was torn down at the beginning of the present century (its former site is now occupied by the Hotel Palace and the well-loved Iglesia del Cristo de Medinaceli). The present Duchess resides in the Casa de Pilatos, which has been superbly restored. Also preserved for posterity are the documents in the family's archives dating back a thousand years—the most important private collection of its kind in Spain.

The large plaza outside the main entrance of the palace is, in reality, the first of three patios, each more elaborate than the last, that the visitor will encounter. It was part of the estate and could be closed at night; here were held parties, as well as games, equestrian parades, bullfights, and religious ceremonies, for spectators in the loggias and balconies of the house. From the plaza, one passes under the triumphal portal to enter the courtyard, called the *Apeadero,* which, in the days of horse-drawn carriages, echoed to the splendid racket of iron wheels on cobblestones. Colonnaded galleries giving access to the house provide shelter from the elements, and along the walls are orange trees espaliered in the traditional medieval style, which gave each branch maximum exposure to the sun, encouraging an increased yield of fruit. The trees are shaped to make decorative figures, such as rhombuses and candelabra. Bougainvillea, indigenous to Brazil, is presently trained against the walls in the corners of the patio and trails down from the tops of the galleries, filling the bays between the columns with masses of purple bracts in season.

From the *Apeadero* the visitor passes to the principal patio of the house, an imposing space paved with black and white marble squares and enclosed by two lev-

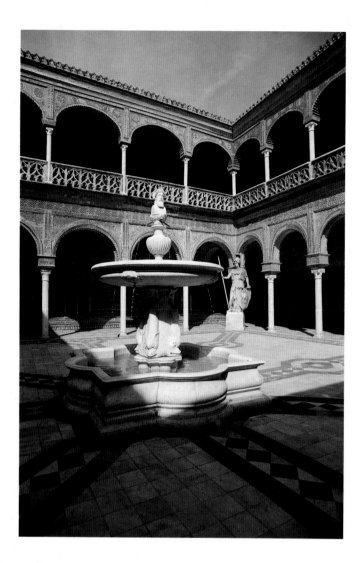

Casa de Pilatos: The principal patio

ABOVE RIGHT
Casa de Pilatos: Minerva

OPPOSITE
Casa de Pilatos: *Azulejos* decorating the entrance to the Jardín Grande

els of galleries. The marble columns that support them are of Renaissance inspiration and carry Mudéjar arches; the balustrade is of Gothic design. The inner walls of the arcade and the rooms at ground level are tiled with the characteristic *azulejos,* or blue tiles, of Andalucía and decorated with the intricately patterned stucco known as *yesería.* In the center is a fountain, made in Genoa, topped by a bust of the Roman god Janus, and in each corner a classical sculpture of monumental proportion.

The visitor finds two gardens off this patio: the Jardín Grande and the Jardín Chico. The larger one, to the northwest, the descendant of the primitive Ribera *huerta,* forms a rectangle, incomplete in one corner. At either end, Tortello placed loggias for the display of the sculpture collection; on one of the long sides was constructed a *cenador,* a single-story, colonnaded pavilion, with views of the garden. A grid of paths of *tierra de albero,* a yellowish earth also used in bullrings, forms eleven smaller rectangles; these divisions contain plantings in the Romantic style of 1850 bordered with hedges of Japanese euonymus *(E. japonica).* The following species can be found here: windmill palms of surprising height for their age, date palm, thread palm, sentry palm *(Howea Forsterana),* and southern magnolia; at a lower level one encounters, as an echo of the *huerta* that was once on this site, Seville orange trees, lemon trees, and banana plants *(Musa x paradisiaca).* The red masses of bougainvillea *(B. x Buttiana "Crimson Lake")* are spectacular, as are the Spanish jasmine *(Jasminum grandiflorum),* the yellow-flowered *Jasminum fructicans,* and the Chinese wisteria *(W. sinesis).* Roses ramble along the ground, interspersed with Kaffir lilies and varieties of garden cannas *(C. x generalis).*

In the nineteenth century, an arbor of wrought iron was erected over the Italianate fountain to form a *glorieta* in the middle of this garden. Along with the four

Casa de Pilatos: The Jardín Grande

marble benches that harmonize with the pedestal and basin of the fountain, this domed frame, covered with a veil of jasmine, is the heart of the garden composition. The exultant floral display is framed by Renaissance façades whose windows are covered with esparto mats that protect the interiors of the palace from the sun's glare. When these are raised at night, fragrances from the garden below penetrate to the deepest recesses of the house.

On the other side of the house, to the southeast, is the Jardín Chico, completed in the early years of the twentieth century. It is noteworthy for its wood-roofed cottage, called a *zaquizamí* (a Granadan Arabic word), whose interior, the Salon Dorado, which houses important pieces of classical sculpture, is as compelling as the view of the garden it affords through the superb *reja*—a wrought-iron screen—of plateresque design. In the garden, it is possible to distinguish four tiny contiguous patios, on different levels, laid out on either side of the *alberca* that draws off water from the Caños de Carmona aqueduct. They are arranged geometrically, with boxwood hedging enclosing plants similar to those of the Jardín Grande: palm, jacaranda, magnolia, cycas, and pink rosebushes. The tiling with *azulejos* and the placing of pots of geraniums common to many an Andalusian home are used to great effect. At the intersections of the paths are more Roman statues, symbols of the ruling family's robust aristocratic lineage that can be traced to the Castile and León of King Alfonso X (1252–84) and the France of King Louis IX (1226–70). One of the most prized treasures kept in the Casa de Pilatos was an urn containing the ashes of the Spanish-born Roman Emperor Trajan (A.D. 98–117), which, through the ignorance of a servant, were scattered on the surface of the Jardín Grande, and so even the very earth is imbued with the pride of Roman heritage. The Casa de Pilatos was designated a Historic Artistic Monument on June 3, 1931.

Casa de Pilatos: The *glorieta* in the Jardín
Grande

Casa de Pilatos: The *reja* in the window of
the Salon Dorado

Los Llanos

Marbella
Countess of Los Llanos
and of Larisch

María de salamanca y Lafitte is by way of being an institution on the Málaga coast. She is the great-granddaughter of the illustrious Marquess of Salamanca (1811–1883), a Málaga grandee, politician, and banker, whose name was linked to the most progressive enterprises of the nineteenth century. Among the Countess's family possessions, the hunting estate in the province of Albacete had been given the name Los Llanos, meaning "the plains," which she used for her home in Marbella, where she has resided for several years.

The Countess is well known for her love of plants and for her garden expertise. After heading the Spanish Red Cross for a number of years, she now serves as president of the Club de Jardines de la Costa del Sol, an organization that she has helped build to its present level of seven hundred members from twenty-eight nations. Besides offering horticultural advice and arranging periodic plant exchanges among members, President Larisch works tirelessly to develop a full program of courses, lectures, garden visits, and contests. Each year, with her board of directors, she visits new gardens before awarding the club's coveted awards. And somehow she has done all this while finding time for her ten children (not to mention nine dogs).

Accordingly, we should not be surprised to learn that María de Salamanca has her own beautiful garden, which she planted in consultation with Gerald Huggan, the British horticulturist who came to Spain from Kenya about thirty years ago to design the gardens for Los Monteros de Golf, one of the most innovative of Marbella's residential developments. He is largely responsible for introducing into southern Spain the African species that are now so prominent in its newer gardens.

The garden at Los Llanos is situated on a rectangular three-acre plot with an incomparable view of La Concha, the mountain that dominates Marbella. A broad expanse of lawn sweeps gently up to the unusually long, low house, which is situated on the highest, northern part of the property. The roof, broad enough to be a plain in itself and distinctively tiled, is more characteristic of La Mancha than Andalucía; its lines seem to echo the great pyramid of rock behind it. On the south side of the house, garden borders frame the great lawn of buffalo grass (Stenotaphrum secundatum), a hardy species used in many of the gardens along the Mediterranean coast of Spain on account of its tolerance of seaside conditions. The problem of incorporating the inevitable swimming pool in the scheme was solved by locating it toward the lower end of the garden, leaving a large open space in close proximity to the open southern façade of the house for children's games.

Many of the more than five hundred species in the Countess's garden are found in these borders, which have been planted with a good eye for blending colors, forms, and textures. In this part of Spain, the conventional herbaceous border combining perennials and annuals, an art in which the English landscape designer Gertrude Jekyll (1843–1932) was the acknowledged pioneer, takes on new meaning with the introduction of exotic species, among which, in the case of Los Llanos, one can list the Philippine evergreen shrub Medinilla magnifica; century plants (Agave attenuata) from Mexico; cockspur coral trees (Erythrina crista-galli) from Latin America; peacock flowers (Delonix regia) from Madagascar; bauhinias from China and India; bugloss (Echium fastuosum) from the Canary Islands; flame trees (Brachychiton acerifolius) from Australia; satin flower (Clarkia amoena) from California; the fuchsia called "the queen's earrings" from Guatemala and Bolivia; yellow, pink, purple, and orange varieties of lampranthus from Cape Province, South Africa; and the luxuriant floral carpet created by the ice plant (Mesembryanthemum crystallinum).

The Countess's exquisite rosaleda, located in front of the house on either side of a path leading to the principal entrance, has a trimmed fence of pompom roses and features, among fifty varieties of mainly white roses, "Snow Fairy," a Spanish variety hybridized by Cipriano Camprubi Nadal in 1963. María de Salamanca's love of roses may be in her blood: her illustrious ancestor the Marquess of Salamanca had notable rosaledas in his gardens at his palace on the Paseo de Recoletos in Madrid and at Vista Alegre in Carabanchel.

OPPOSITE ABOVE
Los Llanos: The house from the garden, with La Concha in the background

OPPOSITE BELOW
Los Llanos: The swimming pool

164

O NE MUST TRAVEL quite a distance from the main coast road to find La Cascada de Camogan, a residential development that, as the name suggests, occupies a rocky spur close by a ravine. A number of gardens in Marbella
incorporate distant views of La Concha, the town's omnipresent mountain. In the
case of the garden of La Sardinella—the name means "little sardine"—the owners
practically scaled its peak.

The house, which is the property of Joseph Magnus Matter, a German-Swiss
banker who resides much of the year in Switzerland, has a far from somber appearance, a circumstance that may be attributed to Wilma Lindomar da Silva, the Brazilian wife of the owner at the time that the house was built. The gay extroversion of,
for example, the bougainvillea-covered walls of pure white stucco and the exterior
stairs to the upper level are indicative of the fact that the Italian architect consulted
Brazilian taste in the design of the house. At least in architectural terms, the average
Spanish householder keeps to himself: traditionally, the *casa* looks inward and
eschews display.

In the generous reception patio in the front of the house, nicely paved with
brick and framed with cypresses, a small, sunken fountain of decidedly Hispano-
Islamic inspiration, marked off with flowerpots of pink geraniums, reminds one that
this is, indeed, Spanish soil. From there the visitor can proceed through an Italianate
arch into an arcaded patio, whose central fountain, a basin raised on a pedestal, suggests that one has traveled back in time to Renaissance Florence. A low wall enclosing the fountain supports poinsettias in pots at the corners. A glance back at the
entrance provides a reassuring glimpse of the mountain's peak, while the view south,
framed by the living room's generous opening onto the canopied sun deck, disclos-
es the swimming pool set in the lawn, its bright blue echoed by the blue of the
Mediterranean in the same plane.

Although, perhaps, more Brazilian than Andalusian in feeling, one of the gar-

LA SARDINELLA

Marbella
Joseph Magnus Matter and
Wilma Lindomar da Silva

OPPOSITE ABOVE
La Sardinella: The reception patio

OPPOSITE BELOW
La Sardinella: The enclosed patio

BELOW
La Sardinella: The garden façade

La Sardinella: The brook

den's most striking effects has been achieved in a broad band of hot color—orange, yellow, pink, and several shades of red—that soaks up the sun on the south side of the house. The raised bed immediately below the terrace, and separated from the lawn by a low retaining wall, is so densely packed with, among other plants, cannas, bougainvilleas, geraniums, and marigolds that one might not know that they had any leaves at all.

To the east of the big, raised lawn and screened from the house above by a row of avocado trees *(Persea americana)* underplanted with poinsettias, is a man-made brook, that makes its way over a picturesquely graduated series of rocky steps into a pond in the southeast corner of the property that is a paradise for frogs. An attractive accompaniment to the flowing water is provided by ground cover, mainly of the purslane family, such as portulaca *(P. grandiflora)*, whose flowers open only in direct sunlight. Nearby is a collection of indigenous and long acclimated exotic fruit trees, including cherimoya, coconut, apple, orange, and olive trees, remnants of an orchard that once occupied the site.

In its setting in the shadow of La Concha the pond, with its rustic bridge and postage stamp of an island, could not be more unexpected. Amid water lilies, weeping willows, and agaves, the visitor may be momentarily disoriented—an experience that is not irrelevant to the art of gardening, for a garden is always a space of fantasy.

La Sardinella: The pond

La Dacha

Marbella
Denise and Sioma Schiff

La Dacha: The garden

L A DACHA, WHICH is Russian for a place in the country, is reflective of the increasingly cosmopolitan nature of the Costa del Sol, with its many seasonal houses built by foreigners who spend part of their year in Spain. The house, perched atop a steep hill with breathtaking views of the distant Mediterranean, was designed by a Spanish architect. The man who built it is Russian, his wife was born in Canada, and the man whom this couple commissioned to produce some of its most striking garden features is a British horticulturist who lived and worked in Kenya. The original planting of the roughly three-acre site was entrusted to a local nurseryman in 1983, but it was redesigned some three years later by Gerald Huggan, whereupon, in 1987, it promptly won the prize conferred by the Club de Jardines de la Costa del Sol for the garden with the best botanical varieties. The garden is still years away from assuming the shape it has been designed to grow into.

Thanks largely to Huggan, the well-modulated palette of the mixed border, which is essentially an English contribution to gardening, has been modified in many gardens on the Costa del Sol by exposure to an exciting range of species and varieties. Now this innovative horticulturist sometimes finds that it is all he can do to satisfy a taste for the exotic that he largely helped create. Clients have a way of expecting instant gardens deploying bold effects, and in Marbella's prevailing climate the promise can be fulfilled in the most spectacular fashion.

At La Dacha, what immediately strikes the visitor who has followed the corkscrew drive up to the house, is that in spite of the sweeping view from the ter-

race to the south it is virtually impossible to see the major part of the garden below. Similarly, in the principal area of the garden, a funnel-shaped lawn enclosed by beds of flowers, shrubs, and trees, one can barely see the roofline of the house rising above the broad bank on which Huggan, assisted by two full-time gardeners, maintains lavalike flows of color. The steep hill has been made negotiable by means of a narrow, serpentine path that confers privacy on the stroller and provides fresh impressions at every turn.

How does one begin to describe the plantings? Of trees, for example, there is a small grove—where most gardeners would be proud of a single specimen—of *árbol botella (Chorisia insignis* and *C. speciosa),* with their spiny trunks and large flowers, set in an oval lawn on the southern flank of the hill. Elsewhere on the slope one finds Cape chestnut *(Calodendrum capense),* a native of South Africa; jacaranda *(J. mimosifolia),* whose blue flowers precede the growth of leaves; moss locust *(Robinia hispida);* the so-called love tree *(Cercis Siliquastrum);* and fast-growing rosewood *(Tipuana tipu),* which is often found in coastal gardens. Of special note is a Spanish fir, a protected species indigenous to the Serranía de Ronda, the mountains about fifty miles inland from Marbella.

The visitor will take note of the poetic use of contemporary sculpture in the garden, particularly pieces by Alfaro and Elena Lavaron, but the true horticulturist may be more impressed by the produce garden and the carefully tended compost heaps in a concealed corner of the property: here is evidence of true gardening spirit!

La Dacha: The garden

ESTEPA, MEANING STEPPE, is the name given to the land, high in salt content, through which the Río Genil flows and hence, by association, to the Andalusian town of Estepa, near Osuna, which was captured by Ferdinand III from the Moors in 1240. In 1560, Philip II conferred the title of Marquess of Estepa on Marcos Centurion, an admiral, and, in 1727, Philip V named the sixth Marquess a grandee of Spain. By transfer of title from his father, Iñigo de Arteaga, Duke of El Infantado, Borja de Arteaga y Martin is the fifteenth member of his family to hold it. The Marchioness of Estepa, his wife, is Carmen Fierro y Jiménez–Lopera, daughter of Trinidad Jiménez–Lopera de Fierro and Alfonso Fierro, owners of La Mirada, in the Puerta de Hierro section of Madrid.

It is as much in its arrangement of interior garden spaces—the ubiquitous patios that are here treated with originality—as it is in the fluid sculpting of the enormous space that flows gently from the house down to the distant sea that Casa Estepa commands the attention of the garden visitor. Of the four garden rooms that seem to mark an intermediate stage between "out-of-doors" and "indoors"—entrance patio, porch, summer dining room, and winter patio—distributed on the four cardinal points and each with its own distinctive selection of plants, the last named is perhaps the most rewarding for students of Spanish garden history and botany alike. Here, arranged around a wall fountain at one end are downy thorn-apple *(Datura Metel "Aurea")*, whose marvelous inverted yellow trumpets give off an intense fragrance that some persons cannot bear, and red angel's trumpet *(Brugmansia sanguinea)*, called *santas noches* in Spain, with hanging flowers of light vermilion veined with yellow and more difficult to grow than other varieties of its species. Both species were discovered in Colombia, the latter, the source of a narcotic used by Andean Indians, by the botanists Hipólito Ruiz and José Pavón on their scientific expedition to Chile and Peru, in 1777, under the patronage of Charles III. The bird-of-paradise plants *(Strelitzia reginae)*, native to subtropical South Africa, called *pájaro de fuego,* or fire birds, on account of their electric orange and blue flowers, are planted in compact groups, contrasting with the enormous leaves of the Chinese taro or elephant's ear plant *(Alocasia cucullata)*. A window is framed by the spectacularly beautiful climber *Thunbergia mysorensis,* from India.

The landscaping of the five acres of exterior space is no less striking than the handling of the patios. In an area in which real estate is prized for its relative proximity to the sea, Gerald Huggan designed a garden that flies in the face of convention. What is so daring about his garden design, one of his first commissions on arrival nearly thirty years ago from his adopted Kenya, was his resolute refusal, against all expectation, to include the much-prized Mediterranean in his garden picture. Following a serpentine course, a wide, green river of lawn meanders from the house toward the sea, between plantings of trees, shrubs, and perennials, including a number of the plants, imported from Africa, that have become, in subsequent gardens, this designer's signature. The garden provides a perfect demonstration of the English concern with pictorial values in landscaping, in the manner by which, through a deceptively naturalistic design, one is continually presented with fresh vistas at every turn. From the area in the immediate vicinity of the house it is possible only to hear the distant sound of the waves, muffled by cypresses (x *Cupressocyparis Leylandii)* that boldly interpose themselves between the visitor and the beach.

CASA ESTEPA

Marbella
Marquess and Marchioness of Estepa

Casa Estepa: The winter patio

RESIDENCIA COCA

Marbella

Silvia Moroder de Coca

JUST OVER THIRTY years ago, when Silvia Moroder, with Ignacio Coca, her late husband, first selected a six-acre site for their summer house on property belonging to the Coca family, she was excited to find growing wild on the fine, deserted beaches white flowers like lilies, which she soon naturalized on a small dune below the house that the couple built on high ground set back from the sea. In this spot, amid century plants *(Agave ferox)*, crown-of-thorns *(Euphorbia Milii* var. *splendens)*, and Barbados aloe *(A. barbadensis)*, they make a little flowering cloud, while they have long since disappeared from the now heavily frequented beaches. She also gave a place of honor in her garden to the indigenous European fan palms that she found growing on the dunes and that are so evocative of the sparse vegetation that is still remembered by those who knew the Costa del Sol in the 1950s. The magnificent specimens that one finds in the Coca garden today have not been disfigured by the harvesting of their edible hearts and seem to stand for a time before the Costa del Sol was overdeveloped.

Having built the house and thrown around it a protective screen of blue gum and cluster pine, the owners were then faced with the task of creating a garden on the steep, sandy embankment and the undulating dunes of the low coastal shelf between the house and the beach. Guiding the lady of the house in this difficult task were a profound knowledge of plants and an inherited green thumb, or should we say, green blood, for perhaps the blue blood flowing unquestionably in her veins has changed color! Both her mother, Manrique de Lara de Moroder, and her grandmother, a connoisseur of plants, lived their entire lives on the family estate on Gran Canaria, in the Spanish Canary Islands. From earliest infancy, Silvia Moroder explored at will the fantastic valleys and mountains of the property and got to know and love its luxuriant flora.

Before she could attempt to recreate this paradise on the Costa del Sol, Silvia Moroder had to cover the terrain with a layer of topsoil. The sandy shelf behind the low dunes was seeded with buffalo grass *(Stenotaphrum secundatum)*, in preparation for the garden's striking grove of palms, whose tops, stirring in the breezes off the sea, reach up to the level of the terrace from which the garden visitor first beholds them. Silvia Moroder knew very well that in the green oasis she wanted to create by the sea, palms and yuccas would stand the best chance of surviving. The proof of that wisdom is to be found, thirty years later, in the maturing date palms, European fan palms, spineless yuccas *(Y. elephantipes)*, Spanish bayonets *(Y. aloifolia)*, and the four desert fan palms that form a veritable entrance portico to the grove at the bottom of the stairway to the terrace of the house.

After planting the palm grove, Silvia Moroder turned her attention to making a garden on the bank itself and in the beds that border the lawn. Not surprisingly, one finds here many of the plants that she first got to know and love in her childhood home in the Canaries. Traditional flowering shrubs like rose of Sharon *(Hibiscus syriacus)*, Chinese hibiscus *(H. Rosa-sinensis)*, cotton rose *(H. mutabilis)*, and common rose mallow *(H. Moscheutos)*, with their blazing pink, red, white, and yellow flowers, are interplanted with butterfly bush *(Buddleia Davidii "White Profusion"* and *"Empire Blue")* and such striking plants as Indian-shot *(Canna indica)*, introduced to Europe from Central America in the second half of the sixteenth century; chenille plant *(Acalypha hispida)*, a native of Java, with its velvety red flowers; bird-of-paradise *(Strelitzia alba)*, with strange, almost black and white flowers; and cheriman *(Monstera deliciosa Liebman)*, whose indescribably delicious fruit is enveloped in enormous waxy greenish white flowers. One also finds yellow sage *(Lantana Camara "Mista")*, popular in Spain perhaps because its mixed red and yellow flowers have been interpreted as Nature's salute to its national colors (the plant is known affectionately as *banderita*, or little flag), and, to neutralize its hot colors, the silvery green tree germanders: *Teucrium fruticans*, with pale blue flowers, and *T. canariense*, the red-flowering species from the Canary Islands. Flowers include varieties of the tawny daylily *(Hemerocallis fulva)*, belladonna lily, and African lily *(Agapanthus africanus)*.

One of the most interesting importations from the Canary Islands—from Las

OPPOSITE ABOVE

Residencia Coca: The palm grove

OPPOSITE BELOW

Residencia Coca: The stairs descending to the grove

Palmas—is a well-developed specimen of the African tulip tree *(Spathodea campanulata)* from Gabon, where it is a source of wood for making drums. One of the most beautiful trees in the world, its crown is in summer inflamed with orange flowers that seed the ground beneath it.

Having the sea as a border of one's own garden stimulates a subconscious association with the idea of an island paradise. For more than twenty-five years there was no fence between the garden and the beach: in the farther reaches of the palm grove, there was a large swimming pool with cabanas, and just a few footsteps would suffice to take the swimmer from salt water to fresh water. There are golden dreams that become reality.

Residencia Coca

THE PRINCESS ANNA Maria von Bismarck is famous in the garden world of Marbella for her love of flowers, particularly roses, for which she has a passion. Having won the majority of horticultural shows in which she has exhibited this "queen of flowers," she is acknowledged to be the queen of roses. Her reign began a number of years ago, when she staked out for herself a plot in what is now the most sought-after section of Marbella, which lies between the highway and the shore. In the process, she succeeded in attracting to the town a number of other important people, who have helped give it its undeniable cachet. Next door to Princess Anna Maria lives Prince Alphonse von Hohenlohe.

The residence of Princess Anna Maria consists of a series of cottages, all within a short distance of one another and separated also by clumps of trees and bushes, which help provide a screen of privacy from the nearby road. Intersecting paths of reddish flagstones set in the neatly cut grass link the cottages, which, in their air of playful rusticity remind the visitor of the Hameau in which Queen Marie Antoinette played dairymaid toward the end of her reign. Taking care not to miss one's footing on the narrowly set paths and step on the meticulously maintained lawn, the visitor leaves the reception area bounded by the cottages and sets off in the general direction of the Mediterranean, a journey that can pleasantly fill an afternoon.

On the way, one can pause to admire the plants that are given shelter from the wind and sun on the veranda of the long, low building to one side of the garden, in which the Princess receives visitors amidst her famous floral arrangements. By climbing the outside staircase to the upper deck, one can get a better view of La Concha, which frames the landward view of the garden, and, turning south, be intoxicated by the garden fragrances that are carried on gentle sea breezes.

CASA ANNA MARIA

Marbella
Princess Anna Maria von
Bismarck

Casa Anna Maria: The garden; looking toward the Mediterranean

From the immense lawn and depending on the season, the visitor can admire the planting of the simple mixed borders in which, thanks to the year-round attention of the Princess's four gardeners, each bloom looks like, and probably is, a prize winner from one of the local horticultural shows. Among the vivid floral colors competing for attention may be observed the bright red of Indian-shot *(Canna indica)* and the intense blue of delphinium; the soft pink of the belladonna lily and the faded blue of *Agapanthus campanulatus*; the many colors of the flag irises *(I. x germanica)* and the Spanish irises *(I. Xiphium)*. The way is made pleasant by a number of trees and shrubs, which have been planted either for shade or beauty or both. One finds, among the predominant indigenous Mediterranean species, the so-called *acebuche,* or wild olive. Others, like good tourists, come from remote countries and are on their best behavior in Spain. From China and Malaysia come the dwarf white bauhinia *(B. acuminata)* and the pink, late-autumn-flowering butterfly tree *(B. purpurea).* Also flowering in autumn, with enormous pink flowers, is the *árbol botella (Chorisia speciosa),* which, before it matures, is content to produce only threatening thorns on its trunk and whose silky seed floss is used for stuffing pillows in Latin America.

Finally, in this cornucopia of horticultural delights, we should note the presence of the chalice vine *(Solandra maxima),* a strange plant that belongs to the same family as the potato, tomato, eggplant, tobacco plant, and red pepper; its flowers are beautiful yellowish trumpets with purple lines and the slight fragrance of apricot.

Casa Anna Maria

Casa Anna Maria: A view toward the cottages with La Concha in the background

PATIO, PALACIO BENAVENTE

Jérez de la Frontera
Manuel de Domecq–Zurita

THE CITY OF Jérez, famous for its sherry and its horses, was taken from the Moors in 1264 by King Alfonso X of Castile and León. It was he who granted a tract of land in the city to the Cabeza de Vaca y Benavente family in the aftermath of the Reconquest. This land later passed to the Zurita–Haro family and then to the family of the Marquess of Campo Real, in whose possession it remains.

The Palacio Benavente, in the oldest quarter of Jérez, is a prototype of the Andalusian noble town house, a mansion of many rooms centered on a patio, with wine cellars and stables, a chapel, and gardens. Completed in 1545, the palace was subsequently restored in the sixteenth, seventeenth, and eighteenth centuries. The patio, which gives light, coolness, and tranquillity to the many rooms that open onto it, is Renaissance in style, with carved stone medallions representing virtues of the age, along with busts of the founders of the entailed estate, Pedro de Benavente and his wife, Beatriz Bernalt y Virués, from Segovia, inset between the arches of the colonnaded galleries that enclose it. As in many private patios the earth of this rectangular space was paved over with terra-cotta tiles in the nineteenth century. The central fountain consists of a low, octagonal white marble basin of Islamic origin in which is set a pedestal in the Romantic style.

Two very tall windmill palms, which reach up to the sky from either side of the fountain, are the only permanent plantings in open earth. Scattered about the patio in flowerpots and planters are species that in the nineteenth century, when they were the height of fashion, were considered truly exotic: Kaffir lily, ceriman *(Monstera deliciosa),* and geraniums *(Pelargonium zonale).* Thanks to the climate, these did not become indoor plants in Andalucía, as they must be in most of the rest of Europe and North America.

The palace gardens, created on two levels in 1630, comprise about a third of an acre. The ancient *huerto* only recently lost its original function as a produce garden when it was converted to another use. The Palacio Benavente was declared a Monument of Cultural Interest in 1990.

Patio, Palacio Benavente

THIS HILL OF dreams, a green eminence overlooking the broad floodplain of a river that winds its way toward the Mediterranean at its narrowest point, was purchased by its present owner the very afternoon that he first spotted it. With its prospect of the Rock of Gibraltar and, on clear days, the coast of North Africa, where he also likes to spend time, the hill gave its new owner a foundation on which to build for his sole enjoyment La Villa de las Sirenas. It is here that, in the twentieth century, the style of the Renaissance has been revived—not to mention princely power!—and Mannerism is reborn to open one's eyes wide with wonder.

The way up to this magical kingdom begins, unpromisingly, in the dusty main street of the somewhat neglected village at the foot of the hill. At a distance, it is possible to catch a glimpse only of the palace's cupola outlined against the sky behind a screen of Italian cypress *(Cupressus sempervirens "Stricta")*. The entrance to the estate is guarded by two sphinxes, positioned on gate piers. These legendary beasts, half human, half lion, invented by the ancient Egyptians and given the head and breasts of a woman by the ancient Greeks, were much used in gardens of the Baroque and Neoclassical periods. Here, they foreshadow the mysteries of the private world within, which are not even hinted at by the broad dirt road that curves for three hundred feet between a double avenue of Italian cypress underplanted with blue-flowering Cape leadwort *(Plumbago auriculata)*.

From this dark tunnel the visitor emerges into a great square, with a large square pool set in a central lawn, in front of the east wing of the villa, one of several imposing formal areas that have been laid out in the immediate vicinity of the owner's residence. Passing under the eponymous sirens over the linteled entranceway, the visitor walks round the southeast corner of the building and finds a grassy terrace, dotted with Italian stone pines, from which the high-domed, Renaissance-style palace, with its terra-cotta roof tiles specially made to resemble fish scales, can be taken in. There are also breathtaking views south to the distant sea.

LA VILLA DE LAS SIRENAS
Costa del Sol

La Villa de las Sirenas

La Villa de las Sirenas: The *rosaleda*

The owner designed the villa from the inside out, and in order to help him give form to his fantasy he employed Cervantes Martínez, the architect, who was responsible for building the palace, while the fantastic statues ornamenting it were created by Zev, an American architect living in Rome, and by Christopher Hobbs, the sculptor. At the roofline the signature sirens again make an appearance. These mythological, fatal songstresses—half woman, half fish—symbolize the desires that can never be satisfied.

The creative team cited above was also employed in the making of the architectural and sculptural features that greet the visitor in the gardens on both the north and south sides of the long east-west axis of the villa. The motif of the square, introduced in the entrance plaza, is repeated throughout, and as at Versailles, stairs are used to create chimerical perspectives that seem to expand the space of the gardens beyond their physical borders.

The visitor may begin in the *rosaleda,* to the west of the palace, dedicated to Diana, goddess of the moon, and planted, appropriately, with only white roses. Here, an arcane mythological program turning on the themes of duality and transformation, and appropriate to a garden of Renaissance inspiration, is introduced by the white marble serpents that decorate the central fountain. Stairs descend to a broad walk, nicely made with rowlock brick and screened by trees from the terrace above, that affords two of the garden's most breathtaking spectacles.

Suddenly, one finds oneself looking out over the surrounding landscape to the Mediterranean on the horizon from the top of a steep flight of stairs that sweeps down to a long lawn, both framed with cypresses underplanted by masses of white oleander *(Nerium Oleander "Album")* and white spirea *(Spiraea albiflora).* Resisting the temptation to descend and instead turning back to the brick walk, one finds one's eye drawn by a narrow, bubbling central channel of water in the direction of the garden's most elaborate and most playful *capricho,* the Nymphaeum, or water parterre.

183

Framed by the arched entrance to this enclosed space can be seen a niche in which a veil of water falls from a height of thirteen feet before a bust of Neptune enlarged beyond all human scale. The mighty god of the sea, his enormous hand resting on the lower edge of the pool that collects the falling water, appears to be on the point of climbing out of the fountain.

Neptune presides over the Nymphaeum, a confectionery arrangement of twisted candy-cane columns and sprouting urns located below the level of the villa to the east. This watery realm of 270 square feet consists of four square pools intersected by balustraded raised paths that meet in the middle. The creators of this extraordinary garden room had to dig to a depth of sixteen feet into the hill in order to achieve the desired effect.

The owner of the Villa de las Sirenas began, in 1974, by first building himself a house, and then the elaborate gardens, to which the most important contributor may have been the landscape architect Leandro Silva Delgado. Both men share a passion for Arabic culture, which is reflected primarily in the choice of the elevated site with its commanding views, the ingenious use of water, and the reliance on traditional Hispano-Islamic garden plants, such as the myrtle. As part of his plan, Leandro Silva has introduced in these continually evolving gardens a variety, impressive both numerically and botanically, of trees and shrubs that provide a green canopy for the palatial hilltop, from which its owner and his guests can enjoy having their gaze directed by stately avenues of trees to the horizon. Finally, perhaps no feature of this fifty-acre estate is quite as audacious as its newest creation, of Islamic inspiration: the *palmeral*, a grove of some two thousand specimens of date palm and desert fan palm interspersed with mimosas.

La Villa de las Sirenas: The view down the cypress allée toward the Mediterranean

OPPOSITE
La Villa de las Sirenas: The stairs leading from the *rosaleda*

185

La Villa de las Sirenas: The terrace walk
leading to the Nymphaeum

La Villa de las Sirenas: The Nymphaeum

OPPOSITE La Villa de las Sirenas: The Neptune fountain

La Majada del Lentisco

Sotogrande
Mary Melian Zobel

La Majada del Lentisco

AJADA IS AN old Castilian word of Latin origin that derives its meaning, a shelter for shepherds and their flocks, from the mesh or netting that was used to secure the sheep. The lentiscus, or mastic tree *(Pistacia Lentiscus)*, has long been indigenous to the Mediterranean region. Its fine resin, called mastic, was known to the ancient Greeks. This interesting tree formed part of the aboriginal vegetation on the primitive *cortijo* where the late Alfredo Melian Zobel, Sotogrande's pioneer developer, settled before transforming it into a fashionable resort.

The house that he built, the first in Sotogrande, was completed in 1966. It has the amplitude and grace that one associates with upper-middle-class life at the end of the last century. With its high ceilings, vertical windows, and wrought-iron balconies, expressive of the ambience of maritime Andalucía, it is not unlike the colonial mansions that were in vogue at the turn of the century in such places as Tangier, Havana, and Manila (the Melians maintain strong ties to the Philippines, where they lived for a number of years).

The two-acre property is bordered on the east by a golf course, which is a most effective way to increase the apparent size of a plot of land. The historically and environmentally responsible decision to preserve the indigenous cork oaks permitted the very private family to interpose between their house and the road a seemingly impenetrable barrier, through which the visitor is obliged to tunnel up a steep drive. It would not be an exaggeration to call the Majada del Lentisco a cork oak grove enriched with other plants, for this acid-loving, ancient inhabitant of southern Spain and North Africa—the traditional source of cork obtained by periodic stripping of its wrinkled bark—is well established here. These trees provide much needed shelter for the lovely gardens that Mary Melian Zobel, the lady of the house, has created. Born a Randolph, one of the first families of Tennessee, Mary Melian has brought to this part of southern Spain, a region that is also famous for both its courtliness and its charm, the gracious touch of the American South.

Beneath the wide tops of oaks, the garden plants prosper, among them the strawberry tree, myrtle, alder buckthorn *(Rhamnus Frangula)*, rosemary, butcher's broom *(Ruscus aculeatus)*, rock rose *(Cistus salvifolius)*, broom, Spanish lavender *(Lavandula Stoechas* subsp. *pedunculata)*, heather, heath, jasmine *(Jasminum fruticans)*, and, of course, the mastic tree. Lawns bordered with these plants lead the visitor through a discreetly hidden open-air pool room, complete with a small, distinctively Philippine pavilion. The Casa de Nácar is named for the translucent chips of mother-of-pearl, or *nácar*, arranged like fish scales in panels framed by dark wood from which it is constructed. Farther on is a sloping garden area enclosed by holly oaks and cypresses and planted, by landscape gardener Russell Page (1906–1985), with a beguiling and characteristically quixotic combination of flowers, shrubs, and herbs, among them roses, tomatoes, pomegranates, oregano, chives, carnations, orange trees, and violets. Here, in the month of May, the "rose beds for Mary," as Page called them, produce a mass of mainly white blooms.

At the opposite end of the garden, close to the house, Canary Island date palms anchor the long lawn that runs the full length of the terrace, where family meals are served beneath a pergola supporting a Concord grapevine salvaged from an old Málaga hotel. In a salute to the American South of Mary's childhood, a white hammock slung between two holly oaks invites repose.

Of the two superbly beautiful, and strikingly different, patios created by Mary, the larger, adjoining the vestibule and the living room and walled off from the garden, to which there is access by a wrought-iron gate set in an arch, is more in keeping with the colonial atmosphere of the house than with the Roman or Arabic patios that we have seen elsewhere. Cascades of fragrant yellow roses *(Rosa Banksiae "Lutea")* virtually smother a shrine-like wall fountain surrounded by votive pots; these, along with the pure white "Iceberg" Floribunda rose and the intense reddish brown flowered honeybush *(Melianthus major)*, with its attractive foliage and heady

La Majada del Lentisco: The terrace at sunset

perfume, contribute to the fin de siècle charm of the space. White ginger lilies *(Hedychium coronarium)* and white dutchman's pipe *(Epiphyllum oxypetalum)* are grown in beautiful old Spanish ceramic pots.

It is in this patio, as a testament to its creator's knowledge and love of plants, that one finds the best examples seen in any Spanish garden of the dahlia, which first flowered in Spain about two hundred years ago, following its introduction from Mexico, in 1789, to the Real Jardín Botánico in Madrid, where it was first described, one year later, by Antonio José Cavanilles, the Valencian botanist who was the director at the time. In twentieth-century Sotogrande, the gardener is rewarded in December with a marvelous display of pink-lilac flowers twelve inches in diameter.

The smaller of the two patios, at the heart of the house, and accessible only from Mary's bedroom, attractively echoes in its planting the blue of the *azulejos* with which the patio's floor and the adjoining bathroom are tiled. There is yet another little wall fountain; clay pots hold ferns and palms; and bamboo poles laid crosswise on top of the white walls, where white doves perch, support a blue trumpet vine *(Thunbergia grandiflora)* whose flowers rain down into the patio below.

La Majada del Lentisco: Russell Page's
"rose beds for Mary"

La Majada del Lentisco: The small patio

OPPOSITE
La Majada del Lentisco: The principal
patio

VERITABLE GARDENING craze appears to have gripped the leisured set that has put down roots in the Costa del Sol and that has chosen, not always wisely, to take advantage of a beneficent climate by introducing exotic plants that acclimate easily and can be positively breathtaking. Certainly Spanish gardens have been immeasurably enriched by the plants of other continents—who can imagine Andalucía now without its geraniums, which come from southern Africa?—but such new species are embraced by an established culture gradually and selectively. Over the past twenty-five years, thanks to the widespread planting of exotic flora for reasons of novelty, commercial convenience, and ignorance, parts of Spain's Mediterranean coast have come to resemble stretches of tropical forest.

It is therefore all the more astonishing, and something of a welcome relief, to discover, in the colony of Sotogrande, a garden that makes its strong visual appeal by distilling the very essence of all that we may have inherited from our Roman and Arab forebears. The peaceful exterior of Alfonso Zobel's low, white house, built in 1972, viewed from the forecourt planted with white oleander *(Nerium Oleander "Album")* and white rose beds bordered with hedges of myrtle *(Myrtus communis*

PRIVATE RESIDENCE

Sotogrande
Alfonso Zobel

Private Residence, Sotogrande: The small patio

OPPOSITE
Private Residence, Sotogrande: The principal patio

Private Residence, Sotogrande: The
principal patio, viewed from the house

"*Microphylla*"), ought to give us a clue as to the spirit in which this successful busi-
nessman and interior designer has modeled its planted spaces, both within the
house and in the garden to which it leads.

Entering the marble vestibule, the visitor is received by a sphinx into a space
with a small sunken fountain and a single fern that produces a premonitory sensation of perfectionism and hermeticism. To one side of a coolly elegant living room,
imposing double doors of carved oak open into a jewel of a marble patio. In the center of its polished rectangular floor is a fountain of Moorish inspiration, and in the
center of each of its four quadrants, which are marked off by tiny channels emanat-
ing from the fountain, is a hemispherically clipped orange tree. At either end of the
patio, intertwining trunks of *Clytostoma binatum,* a close relation to the trumpet vine
from central South America, are trained up the faces of piers that carry an arcade,
creating, in season, a cornice of mauve flowers.

None of this, however, can quite prepare one for one's first view, from the living room, of the principal patio with its swimming pool. There may be several
lessons to be learned here, not least that a pool, which has become, at least in the
oppressive heat of southern Spain, an indispensable adjunct of the good life, need
not be a distracting afterthought; indeed, it can be the brilliant focal point of a rigorous garden composition, as exemplified in the Patio de los Arrayanes in the
Alhambra. Such discipline is exhibited here that even the oleanders that are in most
seasons the only spots of flower color in this patio, begin to seem intrusively bright.

In addition to its Arabic reminiscences, there is something triumphantly
Roman about the central placement of the long, blue-tiled pool and, of course, in

the massive, museum-quality imperial male bust that commands the inviting water from the security of a plinth in front of the hedge of Italian cypress that borders one of the long sides of the patio. Seated at dusk on the terrace just outside the living room, mesmerized by the gently ruffled surface of the water, the visitor gratefully reviews the upright originals of the forms forever waveringly inverted there: a white wall, warmed by the declining sun, and, at the other end of the pool, a pillared loggia giving access to the garden beyond and framed by three asymmetrically positioned sky-pointing cypresses, one in one corner, and two providing unexpected balance in the other. As night falls, the stuccoed walls glow with color, the water gleams, and the cypresses become watchful black presences.

A terrace just the other side of the loggia that closes off the main patio is planted with Seville orange trees arranged between low boxwood hedges. From here, the steep incline of the terrain necessitated the construction of stairs to the garden below, which was laid out by Russell Page, who came to see the house under construction and, without uttering a word, began to design (his hand may be detected in the planting of the patios as well). Alfonso Zobel's respect for the indigenous vegetation of the scraggy, one-and-a-half-acre plot on which he located his residence is expressed in the thick wood composed of cork oak and holly oak, interspersed with Page's solemn rows of cypress. The brick paths are neatly hedged with abelia *(A. Schumannii)* and the shaded ground is planted with ivy and sword fern *(Nephrolepis exaltata)*. The ensemble gives proof that many varieties are not necessary to form a garden, but rather much art. And that to be original, there is nothing like returning to origins.

Private Residence, Sotogrande: The principal patio, viewed from the garden

Madrid

1. Patio de Los Evangelistas,
   Monasterio de San Lorenzo
   de El Escorial
2. Los Molinillos
3. La Mirada and La Yedra
4. Torrebeleña
5. Calle Turégano, 1
6. El Capricho de la Alameda de Osuna
7. Jardín de El Principe, Aranjuez

Castile

GUADALAJARA
8. Piedras Menaras
9. Real Fábrica de Paños, Brihuega

SORIA
10. Vernacular Garden, Medinaceli

TOLEDO
11. Los Palacios de Galiana
12. Castillo de Layos
13. El Castañar
14. Santa María de las Nieves

SEGOVIA
15. La Granja de San Ildefonso
16. El Romeral de San Marcos

Galicia

PONTEVEDRA
17. Palacio de Oca
18. La Saleta

LA CORUÑA
19. Cloister Garden, Monasterio de
    San Lorenzo de Trasouto
20. Pazo de Ortigueira

Catalonia

TARRAGONA
21. Cloister Garden, Monasterio de Poblet

BARCELONA
22. Cambó Residence

GERONA
23. Hortus Botanicus Marimurtra
24. Santa Clotilde

Balearic Islands

MAJORCA
25. Alfabia
26. S'Avall

Valencia

VALENCIA
27. Monforte

ALICANTE
28. Huerto del Cura

Andalucía

GRANADA
29. La Alhambra
30. El Generalife
31. El Albaicín and the Carmen
    de los Cipreses
32. Carmen de la Fundación
    Rodríguez Acosta
33. Jardines de Narváez

CÓRDOBA
34. Patios, Córdoba

SEVILLE
35. Patio de los Naranjos
36. Patio, Seville
37. Casa de Pilatos

MÁLAGA
38. Los Llanos
39. La Sardinella
40. La Dacha
41. Casa Estepa
42. Residencia Coca
43. Casa Anna Maria

CÁDIZ
44. Patio, Palacio Benavente
45. La Villa de las Sirenas
46. La Majada del Lentisco
47. Private Residence, Sotogrande